REGNUM PRACTITIONER SERIES

The Journey Concept

Series Preface

While we delight to serve the academic community, our mission is to enable the global church to engage more readily in God's mission in its very diverse contexts. To do this we seek to bring practitioners and academics together. Our desire is that this series will bridge the gap that sometimes exists between, on the one hand, Christian leaders and mission practitioners and, on the other, Christian researchers.

REGNUM PRACTITIONER SERIES

The Journey Concept

Rethinking Organisational Strategy in the Global Context of God's Mission

Susan van Wynen

First edition published 2023 by Regnum Books International
in partnership with Wycliffe Global Alliance

Regnum is an imprint of the Oxford Centre for Mission Studies
St. Philip and St. James Church, Woodstock Road
Oxford, OX2 6HR, UK

www.regnumbooks.net

British Library Cataloguing in Publication Data
A catalogue record for this book is available from the British Library

ISBN: 979-8-8898-3899-9
eBook ISBN: 979-8-3419-0000-4

Typeset by Words by Design

Cover image by N. on unsplash.com

All Scripture references, unless otherwise indicated, are from the ESV.

Distributed by Fortress Press in the US, Canada, India, and Brazil

Contents

Acknowledgements

And thus, though Wisdom was Himself our home, He made Himself also the way by which we should reach our home.

Augustine, On Christian Doctrine

Thank you to:

- God for this and so many opportunities to see his love expressed, his Church equipped, and his people finding their way on this journey home.
- Wycliffe Global Alliance Executive Director Stephen Coertze and former Executive Director Kirk Franklin. They dragged me into this, gave me space and grace and encouragement.
- The Alliance leadership team and the many other leaders from around the world who participated in the Journey Survey and who have encouraged this new way of working. The research, the ongoing development of Journey Concept resources and experiences, and this book are only possible because of their willing participation and encouragement.
- My amazing editor Dawn Kruger who, even after editing my dissertation several years ago, was still willing to also edit this book.
- A great group of advance readers who asked tough questions and gave input which helped refine the content.
- My long-suffering husband Tom van Wynen and all my family who keep me as balanced as possible.
- Special thanks to Nelus Niemandt who supervised my PhD studies and dissertation. I could not have asked for a more encouraging advisor.

Descriptionary

Rather than offering definitive statements on terms used in this book, here are a few brief descriptions that may be helpful.

Journey Concept: Our ongoing participation with God in his mission, at his invitation, under his direction. The Christian's life is a journey with God. Similarly, the life of any organisation that desires to glorify God is also a journey and is (or should be) about discerning the path to best participate in God's mission together. The Journey Concept is a mindset, heart change, and ongoing process of aligning with the mission of God for service and blessing. We've never been this way before… but we are not alone.

Mission: "Fundamentally, our mission (if it is biblically informed and validated) means our committed participation as God's people, at God's invitation and command, in God's own mission within the history of God's world for the redemption of God's creation" (Wright, 2006: 22-23).

Missional: Something characterised by mission. An identity and/or role connected to God's ultimate intention of redemption, restoration, and renewal.

Intent: Having one's mind and will focused on a specific purpose.

Missional Intent: Listening, learning, and living the journey of participation in God's mission.

The connecting of our identity (who we are) to God's purposes.

Discerning our part in God's mission.

Committing our hearts and minds to specific areas of focus (how we approach our vision and mission).

A setting of direction, including the concerns, contexts, and/or causes an organisation, group, or individual believes God has called them to. The intent is clear, but the strategies and actions are flexible and constantly attuned to God's leading.

Wycliffe Global Alliance: As a part of the worldwide church and the global mission community, the Wycliffe Global Alliance is a community of more than

100 diverse organisations and networks serving together in Bible translation movements around the world.

Introduction

The Christian's life is a journey with God. Similarly, the life of any organisation that desires to glorify God is also a journey and is (or should be) about discerning the path to best participate in God's mission together. This is the Journey Concept.

The journey concept, as both metaphor and reality, has the potential to help leaders in multi- and intercultural mission and church contexts develop theologically and missiologically grounded approaches to organisational thinking and planning. It can also help leaders navigate today's complex and shifting contexts. You are invited to consider changes in mindset, vocabulary, attitudes, and actions. Along the way, you'll have the opportunity to reflect on insights, experiences, and the wisdom of mission and church leaders from around the world.

This book is written for leaders and their colleagues in mission and church contexts, as well as for businesses, movements, networks, and other organisations seeking to follow Christian principles. It's also for the individual who just wants to explore what it means to journey with God as part of the worldwide church.

Let the adventure begin!

Contemplating a Journey with God

Why the journey concept? Learning about journey through Scripture, church history, literature, and a myriad of cultural contexts offers a new way of looking at strategic thinking and planning. A journey is a holistic undertaking. To prepare and travel well, we need to consider many factors: purpose, leadership, followership, climate, terrain, context, resources, travelling companions, time, space, milestones, history. The journey concept includes metaphor but is more than metaphor. It is reality. Life is a journey. Many metaphors can be tools for energising and motivating organisational planning. However, living out the reality of the journey requires a new kind of commitment and a new way of seeing and being. It offers a different starting point for approaching problem-solving, discernment, decision-making, and direction in Christian organisations.

For leaders, contemplating such a journey puts the focus on calling and context rather than on control. Christian organisations need a solid theological and missiological core. From this core flows missional intent. Missional intent is the connecting of our identity (who we are) to God's purpose of blessing the nations. It involves focusing our hearts and minds on a specific purpose or purposes (how we approach vision and mission) according to his leading. Missional intent is about setting direction in keeping with who God has called us to be and what he has called us to do. It means embracing the concerns, contexts, and/or causes God sets before us as an organisation, group, or individual. Discerning our organisation's missional intent is not the same as making a five-year strategic plan. It is an ongoing process of discovery. It is listening, learning, and living the journey under God's direction.

The journey concept grew from a need for something beyond traditional strategy models. I have had the privilege of being part of the leadership team of the Wycliffe Global Alliance since the Alliance's beginning, more than a decade ago. In the early days of our formation, our executive director Kirk Franklin asked me to consider how we should think about and approach strategic planning. I'd worked in this area before, but as I reviewed classic literature and current resources, nothing seemed to fit. The journey concept emerged out of that void and in reflection on global realities, our own contexts, and our quickly changing and growing global network of local organisations. The concept resonated with our leadership team. It had the potential for theological and missiological development and applications. It also seemed to fit with the values of flexibility, cultural diversity, unity, and the sense of community and collaboration that Alliance leaders were seeking to make a vital part of the Alliance culture.

Journeying in community

Preliminary discussions with colleagues from multiple cultures offered a glimpse of the richness and diversity found in the concept of a journey. This was an important factor as we were working on moving beyond our organisation's primarily Western-dominated past. Further encouragement came from a workshop on journey-based planning held in Africa with colleagues from around the continent and, later, in the Americas, an organisational review process using the journey concept (see this and other journey case studies in the Appendix of this book and in *A Missional Leadership History*, chapters 11-12). There was a high level of enthusiasm and participation. Some participants expressed great relief at not having to follow traditional planning models and were encouraged by the reminder that leading also involves following and sharing the burdens. Numerous conversations with pastors and leaders from other organisations around the world also revealed an interest in and a basic understanding that the journey concept was more than a theory and could be applied in very practical ways. For example, when I mentioned the journey concept during a casual dinner conversation with a group of South African pastors, one pastor exclaimed, "We need this!" as others nodded. He explained that he had seen African leaders too easily influenced by out-of-context methods and strategies offered by some Western churches and church networks.

Exploration of the journey concept is fruitful for several reasons. Primarily, it fits with the reality of God's mission. As Christians, we are called to participate with God in his mission. We are called to follow him. The "Great Commission" verse, Matthew 28:19, is bookended by verses in which Jesus talks about his authority and presence. He doesn't just give a command and turn us loose. The journey concept is based on a powerful metaphor, but it is also an actual journey in the company of Christ and in the footsteps of Christ. And those footsteps are found throughout the Bible, not just in a few New Testament verses. We have much to learn about participating in God's mission.

A deeper look at the issue of strategic planning is essential to developing a sound theological and missiological core for organisational thinking and behaviour. This book engages with the constantly changing and challenging issues of how organisations (meaning the multitude of people within an organisation) articulate and live out their callings and their participation with God in his mission. This is not something we do alone. We do it as a body, in community. The research that led to this book has demonstrated that the concept of a journey can potentially:

- provide a more biblically and missiologically aligned, helpful, and effective basis for creating new ways of leading and participating in organisational thinking and planning in and among mission and church organisations;
- address organisations' desires to flourish in and respond to the complex local and global environments of today and tomorrow;
- be effective in multicultural and global contexts.

The themes above were addressed through three key areas of research: metaphor and organisational strategy, cultural impressions of journey, and journey and Scripture. This research is informed by the work and journey of the Wycliffe Global Alliance, with much gratitude for the participation of so many leaders. However, the application potential and implications of the research are broader and deeper than the scope of any one group or type of organisation.

The journey's source and substance

Most strategic planning philosophies and methodologies were not created or developed to reflect or support organisational participation in *missio Dei* (God's mission). Many Christian organisations and businesses look to the corporate world for planning models,[1] adapting and adjusting the models to better fit

[1] Note: the deeper that I went into the topic, the more it became clear that "journey model" was not the most helpful term. When I used this term, people had expectations of five-step plans, precise structures, and instructions to follow. The term "journey concept" and talking of it as an "approach" was better understood. People saw it as a contextually adaptable way of perceiving, thinking, and working rather than a set of

Christian values. Or, leaders may adapt and adjust their organisations to better fit the planning models. Well-meaning churches and ministries often adopt traditional strategic planning methods or more recent strategy trends (often as late adopters) out of a desire to be "professional". They maintain their Christian posture in their planning sessions by including prayer and asking God's blessing on their plans.

"Rather than finding biblical legitimation for our activities, we should be submitting all our missionary strategy, plans and operations to biblical critique and evaluation" (Wright, 2006:37). In keeping with missiologist Christopher Wright's statement, we will explore and assess the viability of using the concept of a journey to create an adaptable, innovative approach for strategic thinking and planning in the context of Christian organisations. Observing how Scripture portrays this concept and digging into what it means is essential.

South African missiologist David Bosch spoke of how we "use our prayers merely as gimmicks to obtain divine sanction for our own blueprints" (1991:17). These sound like harsh words because few would admit to doing this intentionally. However, Bosch highlights the dangers of merely adding a spiritual veneer to our own handiwork. His words are a caution to seriously evaluate our motives. Reflecting on Bosch's warning, is the goal to "sanction [...] our own blueprints" and accomplish our own goals? Or do we just not know how to find a path that is better aligned with God's intentions?

Traditional strategic planning was founded on centuries of military strategy, forged in the twentieth century's age of industry, and cheered on in the competitive spirit of game and sport. Many Christian organisations, including churches, still rely on philosophies and methodologies steeped in these influences. These approaches are, however, often at odds with the values and the current and future needs of organisations seeking to participate in God's mission. You can learn more about this in chapter 6, where journey thinking is compared with traditional strategic thinking on crucial leadership issues such as change, complexity, urgency, and success.

This book addresses the organisational need for a theologically and missiologically sound approach to strategic thought and practice in global and local contexts. I am passionate about this topic, but this book would not exist if it relied solely on my passion and thinking. What makes it worth reading are the voices from Scripture, literature, and history, and the voices of more than fifty Christian organisation leaders from thirty-six countries. Through the Journey Survey, these leaders[2] contributed personal and cultural insights and wisdom regarding journey influences, perceptions, and experiences. It was deeply

---

instructions. And I have chosen to describe rather than define the concept. A definition envelops its subject, while a description unfolds its subject with the prospect of further revelation.

[2] In this book, the words "leader" and "participant" are used interchangeably in reference to those who took part in the Journey Survey.

rewarding to see the journey concept show evidence of being globally understood, theologically compatible, optimistically received, and realistically applicable as an approach to strategy in multicultural, ever-changing organisational contexts worldwide. May your exploration be rewarding as well.

Journey on!

1. The Power of Metaphor

If our thinking is ever true, then the metaphors by which we think must have been good metaphors.

*C.S. Lewis, in his intriguingly titled essay "Bluspels and Flalansferes"**

Although it can and will be argued that the journey as discussed in this book is a real journey, it is essential to explore the metaphorical journey as well as the literal. Metaphors influence how we think and behave in all facets of life. Metaphors play a significant role in leadership and in strategic thinking and planning. The use of metaphor has shaped and continues to shape how we think about ministry, mission, organisations, and strategy. Understanding the value and use of metaphor can help us better evaluate and maximise the potential of the journey concept for real-life application. Understanding and reflecting on the influence of metaphor may also reveal some new insights concerning your own organisation, network, or church.

> ***The use of metaphor has shaped and continues to shape how we think about ministry, mission, organisations, and strategy.***

What is Metaphor?

Metaphor joins the uncommon with the common, the less understood with the understood, to create a new understanding. Leaders need metaphor to introduce new ideas, to build a vision for change and the future, and to increase effectiveness in complex or complicated contexts. For our purposes, we will use a broad definition of metaphor. "A figure of speech in which a word or phrase is applied to an object or action to which it is not literally applicable" (Oxford University Press, 2023). The word *metaphor* comes from the Latin and Greek *metaphora*, "transfer" or "a carrying across" in the sense of one word to a different word or one idea to another. A number of other languages use words for metaphor that translate into English as "parable", "comparison", "illustration", or "example". Some metaphorical phrases can be cryptic, unless you know the context. Others, such as "life is a journey", are easily imagined as both figurative and literal.

Early examples

Metaphors introduce us to the richness and complexity of languages, contexts, and cultures. This is relevant to the challenges and opportunities of addressing organisational strategy and planning through metaphors, particularly in cross-cultural and multicultural settings. As columnist David Brooks said, "Metaphors are things we pass down from generation to generation, which transmit a culture's distinct way of seeing and being in the world" (2011: A25).

Examples of metaphor appear worldwide in the earliest surviving literary works. The New Testament's depiction of the Spirit "descending like a dove" (Mt. 3:16; Mk. 1:10) recalls the Genesis 1:2 description of the Spirit of God as "hovering" over a formless world. This indicates that figurative language has aided our comprehension from the literal beginning. Among the many Old Testament examples, Jacob's last words to his sons in Genesis 49 provide a wealth of metaphors as he prophesies the future, depicting his sons as: unstable as water (v.4), a lion's whelp (v.9), a haven for ships (v.13), a strong donkey (v.14), a serpent (v.17), a deer let loose (v.21), and a ravenous wolf (v.27). Jacob also speaks of the coming Christ as Shepherd and Stone (v.24). The extensive use and consistency of metaphorical imagery in Scripture demonstrate that God designed and equipped us to include metaphors as an integral part of our thought processes to help us comprehend and communicate concerning the visible and invisible.

> *God designed and equipped us to include metaphors as an integral part of our thought processes to help us comprehend and communicate concerning the visible and invisible.*

Rock, Shepherd, Bread, Light… if God speaks in metaphors, including in reference to himself, we can assume that metaphors are worthy of our attention and contemplation. Metaphors related to vineyards, trees, branches, and fruit are also common in Scripture and other ancient literature. Even when the message was new, the meaning had instant contextual associations. The consistent use of metaphor in Scripture plays a significant role in drawing the strands of Scripture together across the centuries and in speaking truth through the generations, "bringing with them the whole weight of the biblical witness" (Richards & O'Brien, 2012: loc 921).

The Epic of Gilgamesh, originating in ancient Mesopotamia, is considered the world's oldest known literature, its earliest form dating to the eighteenth century B.C. This Sumerian text is rich with metaphors that are often a part of continuing themes. One theme is that of gateways and doorways. "As if some faces could be doorways into life one has an image of but never sees" (Mason, 1970: loc 506). The oldest known Western literature, Homer's *Iliad*, dated to the eighth century B.C., is known for metaphors and similes that graphically compare characters to objects or animals. The following gives a clear picture of how Achilles felt about Agamemnon. "'Wine-bibber,' he cried, 'with the face of a dog and the heart of a hind'" (Homer, n.d.: 128). Thus, the story of the *Iliad* begins.

Influence and impact

If your early schooling left you with the idea that metaphors were primarily decorative add-ons or worn-out embellishments, it missed something crucial. From the beginning, metaphors have been vital to how we conceptualise and understand our world. The metaphors we choose and the way we think about and express our ideas either help us shape an appropriate response to our context and prepare for the future or leave us at odds with our context and the world at large. As leaders, we are responsible for helping create a landscape, an environment, a narrative that will contribute to the flourishing of people and organisations. Leaders need metaphors, but not just any metaphors.

Language greatly impacts how people think about and carry out strategy. Metaphors have shaped corporate cultures around the world. The frequent use of warfare, sports, and industrial metaphors and idioms has influenced the minds, attitudes, and actions of generations. Hungarian linguistics professor Zoltan Kovecses' research claims that we are "wired" for metaphor and that all of our senses are engaged in the creation and use of metaphor (2015: 32). What sights, sounds, smells, tastes are associated with warfare or sports metaphors? Screams, the smell of blood and sweat, the taste of earth – be it battlefield or football pitch? Is this the landscape or environment we seek to create? Perhaps it would depend on the context. High drama and "fighting words" might be appropriate for a Fortune 500 company facing a hostile takeover. But are military terms the best possible motivators or metaphors for encouraging church partnerships, or for helping global mission organisations discuss principles of generosity?

"[A] metaphor is no argument, though it sometimes be the gunpowder to drive one home and imbed it in the memory" (Lowell, 1868). Metaphors used in political and military rhetoric and discourse have long contributed to shaping thinking and actions. Vaclav Havel's stirring 1990 New Year's presidential speech is an outstanding and appropriate example of the use of industrial metaphors. Read his description of the communist regime from which Czechoslovakia had just emerged.

> The previous regime – armed with its arrogant and intolerant ideology – reduced man to a force of production, and nature to a tool of production. In this it attacked both their very substance and their mutual relationship. It reduced gifted and autonomous people, skilfully working in their own country, to the nuts and bolts of some monstrously huge, noisy and stinking machine, whose real meaning was not clear to anyone. It could not do more than slowly but inexorably wear out itself and all its nuts and bolts (Havel, 1990).

Havel continued his speech, challenging and encouraging the people to take responsibility for their future and closing with, "People, your government has returned to you!" (1990).

In *I is an Other*, James Geary claims that we utter a metaphor about every five to twenty-five words, or about six metaphors a minute (2011: loc 119). That means a large percentage of our communication is in the form of metaphor. The further we look into metaphor, the more we understand its power and potential. Metaphors can bring clarity and focus to otherwise fuzzy concepts. Metaphors can be a keenly precise, economical means of communication. They can focus the participant in a particular direction. Acting as a type of shorthand, they eliminate certain avenues of thought while clarifying another. "[M]etaphor is both detour and destination, a digression that gets to the point" (Geary, 2011: loc 255). This directive quality of metaphor demonstrates an incredible amount of power. Metaphors create meaning and define reality. When you accept a specific metaphor, you align your thinking with what it conveys and shut out other possibilities of what might have been.

Creativity and community

Metaphors also lead to new ideas. Our brains are always prospecting for patterns. Metaphor is not just detection of patterns but also creation of patterns. Journalism professor and editor Jack Hart said, "Metaphor was the clay the great physicists used to mould new theories of the universe. Einstein first talked of trains and clocks, then expanded the images to weave time and space into a single fabric" (2007). As mentioned earlier, metaphors allow us to connect known concepts with those unknown and see something we have never seen before. New concepts and inventions can emerge from the creation of new patterns. New ideas and innovations are essential to leaders and organisations, particularly as they relate to both continuous and discontinuous change. Well-chosen metaphors can play a part in encouraging needed creativity.

> *Metaphors allow us to connect known concepts with those unknown and see something we have never seen before.*

A good metaphor invites shared experience. Shared experience, however, requires shared understanding. Because metaphors are often language-dependent as well as culturally based, it may not be possible to duplicate or reconstruct a metaphor from one language to another. Thinking, metaphor, and culture are deeply connected. If a commonly used metaphor cannot be commonly understood in multiple contexts, it will be of little use in a global environment. Considering context is critical to exploring how metaphors work or do not work across cultures and languages.

There are, however, some metaphors that are considered near-universal. This is the closest we can get to "everyone grasps a similar meaning from this metaphor" without testing the metaphor in every cultural and linguistic community in the world. Commonality of human experience gives us many of the conceptual metaphors considered near-universal or potentially universal (Kovecses, 2015: 6). Globalisation, global communication, and widespread use of majority languages have increased the extent of shared understanding. These factors may contribute to some metaphors' near-universal status.

Robert Frost voiced these thoughts:

> [U]nless you are at home in the metaphor, unless you have had your proper poetical education in the metaphor, you are not safe anywhere. You are not at ease with figurative values. You don't know the metaphor in its strength and its weakness. You don't know how far you may expect to ride it and when it may break down with you (Frost, 1931).

As we look at several specific metaphors, we will see what it means to be "at home" with them as they relate to strategy and missional intent. And we will see where each ride takes us.

Living Your Strategy

Here we see the convergence of our topics – God's mission, our participation, strategic thinking, metaphors, and journey. What landscape, what narrative are we creating for our participation in God's mission? What shapes our corporate culture and environment? Much of it is shaped by the words we use and the stories we tell. Leaders know the value of good stories, but they may not be as aware of the stories their metaphors tell. Contemplating this, and recognising the importance of both metaphor and story, we come to metanarraphors.

What is a metanarraphor and what does it have to do with strategy? The word "narraphor" is credited to theologian and futurist Leonard Sweet. He explains, "[A]t the core of who we are, we crave a narraphor (a story with metaphors that help us understand the world, ourselves, and God better)" (2015: 3). A meta-narrative is an expanded narrative. So, a metanarraphor (referenced by Kok and Jordaan in Kok & van den Heuvel, 2019) is an expanded narrative that includes or is conveyed through metaphor. Religion and theology professor C.J.P. Niemandt states, "Metaphors allow leaders to draw a picture of possibilities. Narratives shape and form reality, give context and imagination to language, and are vital for transformation" (2019a: 193). Metanarraphors open the way for creating new landscapes where leaders and followers can come to new understandings and new, shared points of view.

Metanarraphors are readily visible in advertising because promotion begs for a memorable story. Think about familiar brands and how they have communicated over the years. Are they telling stories that communicate security, edginess, belonging, nostalgia, quality? Are the images and advertisements playful, sentimental, serious, trendy? Have the companies they represent changed their metanarraphor as society has changed? What do their metanarraphors tell you about the kind of audiences or customers they want to attract and keep?

Not all metanarraphors are born in marketing brainstorming sessions. Metanarraphors can also be traced or developed in individual lives, in the history of nations, in the recounting of grand causes. Many emerge from history, bearing a strong resemblance to their context and marked by the era in which they were formed. We will explore, for example, the warfare metanarraphor that grew out of the World Wars era and made its way into the business world. Strategy and its related activities have been subject to numerous metanarraphors. These metanarraphors shaped industry, commerce, science, theology, ministry, and any other field or worldview that has ever considered strategy.

As mentioned in the introduction, numerous factors led us to question how we should approach strategy and strategic thinking in the Wycliffe Global Alliance. Recognising the power of metaphor and the necessity of narrative in making sense of our vision, mission, and purpose, it also made sense to consider some of the metanarraphors of strategy. Frost (1931) spoke of being "at home in the metaphor". Niemandt (2019a: 192) describes narrative and new language as "primary building blocks". As we look at metaphors and narrative, we can think of ourselves as making a home of metaphors, or creating a metaphor landscape, a setting in which we can make meaning. The meaning we make and our subsequent actions are directly related to the metanarraphors in which we choose to live.

Warfare, sports, industry, journey. Three of these metanarraphors are among those most commonly related to strategy. The fourth, journey, is known but not nearly as common. As we look at the journey concept, we will consider it as both reality and metaphor and as an alternative to some of the more commonly used strategy metaphors. We will examine if and how all of these metanarraphors connect with strategy and the mission of God.

Most of these metanarraphors can be connected to specific historical contexts and cultures; therefore we will also look at the culture and context of our time, as an example, to see how they pertain to the Wycliffe Global Alliance. Although we are using the Alliance as the key example organisation, our discussions and discoveries can apply in many contexts.

- What metaphors do you commonly use in your context (in your organisation, team, etc.)?
- Why do you use these metaphors? How do they serve your cause?
- What does your organisation or church's metaphor landscape look like? What is the primary metanarraphor that creates your landscape?

Strategy as war

This is an excellent place to begin because it takes us to the historical roots of organisational strategy. In his book, *Strategy: A History*, British military historian Lawrence Freedman tracks strategy's etymology back to classical Greek, saying that the common reference, through the Middle Ages and into the modern era, was the art of war (2013: loc 130). Freedman covers 4000 years of history with warfare metaphors shadowing strategy from the battlefield to the boardroom. In the latter part of his book, he focuses on the importance of story.

Along with Freedman and many other authors (Terry & Payne, 2013; Gaddis, 2018; Greenwald & Kahn, 2005), business professor and author Henry Mintzberg cites the military origins of strategy. He notes that, according to a loose translation of Sun Tzu's *Art of War*, there was a "director of strategic planning" 2400 years ago (2013: 5). For whatever good it does or doesn't do, the metanarraphor construct of strategy as warfare is extensive. There are targets, tactics, troops to rally, turf to defend, beachheads to establish, shares to capture, and strategies to execute. The word *strategy* only began to be used in Britain, France, and Germany in the late eighteenth century, reflecting Enlightenment optimism that war – like all other spheres of human affairs – could benefit from the application of reason (Freedman, 2013: xiv).

Both David Bosch and missiologist Leslie Newbigin address the use of military language in the church and in mission organisations. Bosch states, "At the World Missionary Conference in Edinburgh [1910], to take but one example, the terms used repeatedly included the following: soldiers, forces, advance, army, crusade, marching orders, strategy, planning, and many more. And even when we do not [today] use this terminology, our conduct often reveals a comparable mentality" (1979: 31). The military terms multiplied during the World Wars and spread through the business community and into missions as many of those who served in World War II became the new wave of missionaries in the 1950s. Newbigin points out, "This kind of language, appropriate for a military campaign or a commercial enterprise, is not appropriate here […] for the mission is not ours but God's" (1995: loc 889).

"This kind of language, appropriate for a military campaign or a commercial enterprise, is not appropriate here […] for the mission is not ours but God's." (Newbigin)

How can you tell if you are living in a warfare metanarraphor? There are many signs, but strategy consultant Mark Chussil (2016) gives an excellent example in the following story. There were fifty executives in an executive education programme. One mentioned that a competitor deliberately tried to damage his company. The facilitator asked the executives how many of them thought a competitor had at some time tried to hurt their business. Fifty hands went up. Then the facilitator asked how many had worked for a company that tried to hurt a competitor's business. Fifty hands were lowered. These executives had taken their battle positions, even when there were no wars, only rumours of wars. Furthermore, they believed the stories they had long been told or that had been not-so-subtly implied through metaphor, although their reality begged to differ. They were trained, culturally conditioned, and now entrenched in strategy as warfare. It was the metanarraphor they inhabited.

Professor Luc Audebrand points out, "While various metaphors have waxed and waned in popularity over the years, the war metaphor still guides strategic management theory, research, and education" (2017:1). He states that a reappraisal of the metaphor is long overdue but is concerned that current reforms in business will not create deep or lasting change if the root metaphors remain unchanged. This is a striking statement on the power of metaphor, particularly the warfare metanarraphor. According to Audebrand, reform is not sustainable if the metanarraphors around the reform are not compatible or supportive.

From books and workshops such as *Guerilla Marketing* (Levinson, 2007) to the popular business books and podcasts of US Navy SEAL officers, the warfare metanarraphor shapes corporate strategy and action and has spread worldwide. The warfare metanarraphor certainly has its place in its own military context and there are many admirable qualities and skills that can be learned from these resources regarding self-discipline, persistence, trial-and-error, and thinking creatively. There is no need to eliminate warfare metaphors altogether, but how much should they shape your thinking, your organisation? How does the warfare metanarraphor align with God's mission, your missional intent, and today's global context?

Warfare metaphors are common in Scripture, so it is possible, if nothing else, to proof-text warfare metaphors into Christian organisations' strategies. Furthermore, biblical texts with warfare references are exceedingly helpful in some situations. The Apostle Paul's many military references and use of military metaphors reflect the context of the Roman Empire (Nell, 2019: 90). Roman soldiers were a constant presence; at that time in history, there was no more obvious model of unity, discipline, alertness, and consistency. Many of Paul's references regard the ethics of military unity and loyalty, not warfare in particular. Theologian Mathias Nell (2019) cites Galatians 5:25, which, in the original Greek, contains a metaphor that translates, "If we live by the Spirit, let us stand in close ranks in a spiritual manner, advancing in a closed battle-line (or phalanx)." A literal translation of στοιχῶμεν would be "to be drawn up in a line", which speaks to the idea of conformity (Danker, 2000: 946). English translations usually use "in step with" or "walk by".

In Paul's writings, other uses of military or warfare metaphors are in the context of spiritual warfare. For example, the Ephesians 6 passage on "the full armour of God" clearly states, "Our struggle is not against flesh and blood, but [...] against the spiritual forces of evil" (Eph. 6:12), and the instructions are to "be strengthened in the Lord" (Eph. 6:10), "stand firm" (Eph. 6:14), and "pray" (Eph. 6:18)! However, there is nothing here saying we should command and control. These examples neither advocate for nor against warfare as a metanarraphor for Christian organisations, but show the complexity of the issue. Warfare looks different in different contexts – ancient Israel, the Roman Empire, on the spiritual battlefield, and in churches and Christian organisations influenced by business-speak and thinking.

Imagine the landscape that you are creating through metanarraphor. Do you want it to look like a battlefield? Battles may need to be fought, but is warfare the overall environment you want to establish as your organisational culture? Is that other church down the street the enemy? Are other organisations potential foes or collaboration partners? Are the people you are trying to reach out to a battlefield target? Will a warfare mentality help you in a multicultural, multilingual, global environment? Probably not.

Strategy in the game

It is difficult to move from a combative mindset to collaboration. So, we are not there yet. It is, however, just a short, athletic leap from warfare to sports. The narraphor of organisational strategy as a sport, competition, or game is almost as popular as the warfare narraphor. It reaches metanarraphor status in the USA. Other countries are also influenced, given the popularity of Western business resources and education. Sports metaphors may vary but are popular almost everywhere and in every language.

In English, there are many sports metaphors, and they are regularly heard in business settings, daily life, and from the pulpit. The ball is in their court, full-court press, slam dunk, under the wire, down to the wire, horses for courses, on the bench, bush league, in your wheelhouse, knocked it out of the park, ballpark figure, covering the bases, touch base, step up to the plate, dropped the ball, goal posts, fumble, game plan, kickoff, level the playing field, end run, beaten to the punch, let your guard down, pawn, stalemate, playing with a straight bat, twelfth man. It is all about strategy, scoring, and winning. What sports terms are used in your context?

So, how does a sports or game metanarraphor match with God's mission, your missional intent, and today's global context? There are enough reasons listed above to discourage the thought – the lack of a universal connection (which game?), the potential for an overly competitive spirit, the us-versus-them, winners-and-losers mentality. There may be appropriate moments for sports metaphors, but we should consider why we are using them and if they serve us well. It is hard to imagine a church or Christian organisation spending all its time on the playing field focused on competing with others. The occasional friendly match may exist, but one should not live in the game. This is the challenge. Most metaphors are good for something, in limited and specific contexts. And many different narraphors can boost a project, a new effort, a team event. But think carefully about metanarraphor. You are creating the landscape you will live in, perhaps not forever, but long enough for that metanarraphor to serve its purpose and influence your organisational culture. Is your desire to create competition or foster collaboration? How does your language reflect this?

> *It is hard to imagine a church or Christian organisation spending all its time on the playing field focused on competing with others.*

Strategy and the big machine

As the science of strategic planning rose to prominence in the business world, it took on the nature of the context into which it was born. The mid-twentieth century was still the industrial age, an era of powerful new machines, production lines, streamlined processes, city skylines on the rise, ever faster and wider-reaching transportation and communication, and sweeping social change.

Strategy metaphors often reflect the era and context in which they were created. Building and construction metaphors tell the story of burgeoning brick-and-mortar financial empires. Production line metaphors tell the story of automation and efficiency. Many people continue to live and work under the influence of strategy related to the big machine (industry), particularly if they serve in institutional organisations.

Just as warfare and game strategy metaphors reflect philosophies of conflict and competition, machine metaphors also reflect a philosophy. They grew out of an age of extreme rationality. There was a process for everything, and that process was enacted according to reason. Reason, supposedly based on logic and science, was often considered the only source of knowledge, judge of values, and guide to action (see the writings of Ayn Rand as an example). Reason was how you determined your goals and was integrally connected to self-interest and the survival of the fittest.

By the 1960s, much of Western society took self-interest to mean "do your own thing" and tuned in to rock 'n' roll, civil rights, and miniskirts. However, the business world continued to apply its principles of reason to building now-burgeoning industrial and financial empires. Henry Mintzberg states, "[A]n emphasis on formal rationality permeates the literature of planning" (2013: 13). Structured, systematic, objective, and logical are all keywords for big machine strategy. Mintzberg argues that this is the "old 'machine' assumption". If every component was produced by a machine and assembled in proper order, an integrated product would appear at the end of the line. "This analogy has influenced some of the most important thinking in the field of planning, and has proved to be patently false. Organisational strategies cannot be created by the logic used to assemble automobiles" (2013: 13).

And yet – well into the twenty-first century – the big machine metaphors live on. Command and control are still significant factors in this mechanistic approach as projects are supposed to move sequentially from one clearly defined stage to the next. We have blueprints, foundations, frameworks, and platforms. We have planning cycles, supply chains, and "climb the corporate ladder". We speak of "structures" and "architecture" that have nothing to do with the office building where we may (or may not) be sitting. Add the elements of input, output, and outcome and we have ridden the whole production line. Employees are cogs in a well-oiled machine. Wheels, gears, pipelines, and conduits keep things rolling, turning, and flowing.

Is a big machine or empire-building metanarraphor compatible with God's mission, missional intent, and our global context? There are building metaphors in Scripture:

> For no one can lay a foundation other than that which is laid, which is Jesus Christ (1 Cor. 3:11).
>
> The household of God [is] built on the foundation of the apostles and prophets, Christ Jesus himself being the cornerstone, in whom the whole structure, being joined together, grows into a holy temple in the Lord. In him you also are being built together into a dwelling place for God by the Spirit (Eph. 2:19-22).
>
> You yourselves like living stones are being built up as a spiritual house, to be a holy priesthood, to offer spiritual sacrifices acceptable to God through Jesus Christ (1 Pt. 2:5).
>
> (See 1 Peter 2:6-7; Isaiah 28:16; Psalms 118:22 for more examples.)

> *We are not empire builders but children of the King and it is the King who is building his kingdom.*

None of these passages seem compatible with the empire-building mentality. These passages and many others focus on what God is building, not on anything we might build. There are many good opportunities to use building metaphors – laying a firm foundation or building on rock rather than sand. As you can see from Scripture, however, it is we who are being built. We are not empire builders but children of the King and it is the King who is building his kingdom. Nor will machine metaphors serve very well. The gears grind to a halt in their inability to express the organic nature of life and relationships. Although the metaphors may be useful in specific contexts, we would not want to make our home in a machine.

Industrial and building metaphors describe substance, structure, stability, and sustainability. These are often desirable traits, but may prove insufficient and outdated when prioritised in current contexts where change, flexibility, and the unexpected are on everyone's mind. Mintzberg talks about the challenges of creative planning when plans are built on already-existing structures and systems (2013: 177). We will discuss the challenges of change and disruption more in later chapters.

The words of French philosopher Jacques Ellul still ring true. "The first great fact which emerges from our civilisation is that today everything has become 'means'. There is no longer an 'end'; we do not know whither we are going. We have forgotten our collective ends, and we possess great means: we set huge machines in motion to arrive nowhere" (1989: 60). As followers of Christ, we know our "collective end" and yet we still tend to jump on the "huge machines", thinking they will help us arrive more efficiently, more effectively. We think we need to arrive in the same manner as "everyone else". But we actually need a better model or concept, rooted in sound theological and missiological principles rather than originating from industry, military tactics, sports, and monetary pursuits. Such a concept could offer opportunity for ongoing theological and missiological reflection, discernment, and application in every facet of an organisation's practices and activities. It could also infuse the organisation's reflections and responses related to current global realities and better equip leaders and organisations for future contexts. The journey concept is a way of approaching these needs. Timothy Tennent speaks of the church living out "its witness in the ongoing tension between the 'already' and the 'not yet'" (2010: 309). This is our journey.

Living the Journey

So, what if we changed our strategic thinking and behaviours to align with a journey metanarraphor? Journey is a common metaphor, widespread in use, and near-universal. It also conveniently overlaps with real life. It is difficult, at times, to distinguish when journey is a metaphor and when it is reality, as you can see below. Common understandings of the word *journey* include:

- a travelling from one place to another, usually taking a rather long time; a trip;
- a distance or course travelled;
- a period of travel;
- passage or progress from one stage to another;
- to make a journey; to travel.

Journey can be a noun or a verb. Other English words or phrases that relate to how we talk about the concept of journey include pilgrimage, following a path or a way, a trip, or peregrination (a less common word today).

Perhaps the most commonly used example of journey as metaphor is "life is a journey". You'll find it in greeting cards, university lectures, and fortune cookies. However, for those of us who are Christ-followers, it is also our reality. Together, we journey through life with God. The concept of journey, both metaphorical and literal, although common, is rich enough to merit further reflection.

> *The journey metaphor may be one of the most valuable, realistic, and truthful means of helping people relate to their context and situation.*

The corporate world is familiar with the idea of being on a journey, but the concept has not been developed as significantly as the other metanarraphors we've mentioned. It is often just tossed out as, "We're on a journey" to sum up, downplay, or explain situations not entirely "under control" or times of transition or uncertainty. It "buys time" for figuring out more "concrete" answers as leaders scramble to determine what's next. The irony is, the journey metaphor may be one of the most valuable, realistic, and truthful means of helping people relate to their context and situation. It's not a stop-gap space filler but a description of our ongoing reality.

We need to understand God's mission, our organisation's identity, and what it means to follow. The corporate world produces volumes on leadership, but less on followership. If our journey is to follow God's leadership as he accomplishes his mission and allows us to participate, we have a very different story than the one told in the secular business environment. Moreover, if we are part of a multicultural, multilingual body or organisation, we also need to explore the potential of our metaphors across borders. We have already considered some limitations of various metaphors, particularly the warfare and sports metaphors.

What does a journey metanarraphor look like? Common connections come to mind – paths, waterways, compasses, maps, companions, gear, weather, etc. We will explore how some of these can be useful. However, there is a much wider variety of possibilities.

An example of this is seen in Niemandt's article, "Narraphors in missional transformation of South African denominations". In his research, Niemandt asked denominational leaders, "Can you recall/mention any narrative or metaphor used by leadership to facilitate this [missional] transformation?" (2019b: 193). Those mentioned included: Kingdom of God, taking light to the community, footsteps of Christ associated with the washing of feet, narratives of the traditional missionary (called, sent, preaching, etc.), the road/journey together. Other less common narraphors mentioned were a sailboat, a bridge, and a herd of buffalo. Of the eleven narraphors offered, eight have clear connections to journey. What a rich metanarraphor of the church on a journey arises from such variety of expression! It's easy to imagine how leaders could use most of these narraphors, but the buffalo story was a bit of a surprise, particularly intriguing, and particularly contextual.

For the Cape Buffalo of Kruger Park, South Africa, their life is a life on the move. The herd is constantly moving about and, all the while, some are grazing, some ruminating. Calves are suckling, young bulls playing, drinking, exploring, moving slowly. The leader who provided this narraphor was comparing the buffalo to people in the church, some focused, some not, but all moving in the same direction as a church body (Niemandt 2019b: 193-195). Niemandt cites theology professor Patrick Keifert, who comments that missional change is not linear but follows a somewhat unpredictable path and enjoys multiple causes for each event (2006: 51-59). This speaks to the journey as a metanarraphor capable of dealing with the complexity of change, growth, and surprises.

There is no roadmap

The journey concept is not just another way of talking about a business plan or strategic planning model. Traditional business planning takes a linear approach and seeks to command and control. At best, the plans are made up of a myriad of scenarios (most of which will never happen). At worst, they go into a file drawer and never see the light of day. More contemporary approaches rely on networked and platform models which are often more collaborative, but still with the goal of control. The journey concept acknowledges the mission of God and is a means of talking about and participating in that mission. His people in various configurations (organisations, churches, etc.) follow him with various human leaders who seek, along with colleagues, to discern what God is doing and how they can participate with him.

The word *planning* comes from the Latin *planum,* meaning "flat surface". Planning has been long associated with maps and blueprints drawn on flat surfaces (Steiner 1969: 5; 15). These "flat plans" were considered formal orders to be followed rather than living documents to be adapted and adjusted. The focus of the journey concept, however, is not about documents but about a multi-dimensional way of being and doing life with God and finding purpose as an organisation. There are no roadmaps. Roadmaps may seem an essential part of a journey. Strategic planners often use the idea of roadmaps to help visualise the future and urge people onward. However, in the context presented here, there is no roadmap because we have never been this way before. It is the God who leads us who knows the way. This is a significant difference from traditional organisational thinking.

> *There is no roadmap because we have never been this way before. It is the God who leads us who knows the way.*

As strategic thinking has necessarily shifted away from the "flat plans" and more traditional models, leaders and experts in the business world are also seeking more organic, integrative, and responsive ways to strategise and plan. They are looking for ways to meet the needs of today and tomorrow's multicultural and multilingual global societies, ways to move from competition to collaboration. We will see how the journey concept can be applied and what it might look like as a metanarraphor for meaningful engagement in God's mission and in the world at large.

- How are you currently addressing the changes you see in your context?
- You are on a journey and there is no roadmap. How would accepting this reality change how you approach your organisation's strategy?
- How can metaphors and their accompanying narrative better serve organisations and churches focused on God's mission in today's world and into the future?

2. Journey Perceptions

We will go together.

Journey Survey participant

Journey Questions

To learn more about how people from diverse cultures, contexts, and language backgrounds think about, talk about, and live out the concept of journey, more than fifty Wycliffe Global Alliance leaders from thirty-six countries were surveyed. Overall, there was common understanding of the idea of journey. This brings credibility to the journey concept as an intercultural approach to strategic thinking and planning. However, rooted in that common understanding, there was also a rich diversity of thought and experience, culture and context. Exploring this wealth is a journey in itself – an experience that will enrich our interactions, leadership, and organisations. It would take another book to share all the survey responses. Given the limitations here, I have curated and summarised, but offer direct quotes as often as possible so these voices can be heard.

The Journey Survey questions were:

1. How do you talk about the concept of journey in your language/s and culture/s? What words do you use to express the concept? How would you describe these words?
2. What do you think of when you hear the word *journey* or hear words that express the concept in your language?
3. What feelings and expectations do you have when you think about the concept of a journey?
4. When you think of a journey, do you think of time, distance, or both, or something completely different?
5. What ideas and stories from your culture/s are representative of the concept of a journey?
6. What historical events represent the concept of a journey in your history and culture/s?

7. What are some important aspects of a journey? How important is it to know the destination before you start?
8. How do you think about preparing for a journey? How do you plan, what do you take, do others go with you, and if so, who?
9. Do you think of a journey as cyclical (coming back to your point of origin) or linear? Why?
10. If there are numerous concepts for journey in your language/s and culture/s, what are some of the distinctions?
11. What stories or passages in the Bible that deal with the concept of journey are significant to you, and why?
12. What other thoughts or concepts about the concept of *journey* can you share?

The first two survey questions may have been the most difficult for many participants. One of the most significant challenges was for these leaders to think about the concept of journey in their language, culture, and context, and then write about those thoughts in English. They rose to the occasion and communicated a wealth of information.

The Journey Expressed

Looking at leaders' responses by region helps us see patterns or themes that might not be otherwise apparent. The sampling of responses to Questions 1-3 and 8-10 are offered here by region. Responses to Questions 4, 7, and 12 are also included, but not categorised by region. Responses to Questions 5, 6, and 11 are presented in later chapters.

Pacific

"It is water that connects us." It's not surprising that many people from the Pacific thought of boats when they thought about journeys. One leader shared vivid word pictures of canoes propelled by determined, hardworking paddlers, and sailing boats with the wind in their sails. The focus was on travelling together, a specific destination, and the sombre nature of such an undertaking. "[N]o journey is undertaken for leisure."

"[H]unting, fishing, and harvesting trips – the main purpose of this journey is to bring back meat and food for the family and/or community."

Another leader from the Pacific spoke of journey as sometimes connected to death, referencing the accompanying rituals. "When someone dies, he/she is beginning a journey into another realm; [moving] from the physical to the spiritual. This is a journey of no return. It invokes a lot of deep emotion. That person is going to another village."

One leader shared that, before there were Christians in her region, no one travelled unless they absolutely had to. There was great danger and much fear.

Pacific leaders from urban and suburban backgrounds offered a less sombre picture, mentioning journeys for holidays, adventure, and pleasure.

Participants shared a wide range of descriptions of journeys:

One participant stated the importance of going. "It's not a journey if you don't leave."

Another leader mentioned journeys where one has to flee because of a natural disaster, saying there is "no control and you are uprooted" and that there is additional pain and anxiety "because there is a degree of uncertainty and fear of the unknown". Unlike a journey of acquisition, where you set out purposefully with a plan to bring food, wealth, or knowledge back to your community or family, flight is most commonly a journey of desperation and few options. Another participant also talked about instability and insecurity, because "you may not be able to return home".

Regarding planning, Pacific participants said:

"We plan as we go. We are not the type to just sit. I guess you can say we are more hands-on people."

"Finding out if a similar journey has been undertaken by others and learning from their experience. Ensuring the right materials and amounts (tools, equipment, supplies) are gathered and in good condition. Getting the right kind of people (with the right kind of experiences and qualifications) and ensuring they are adequately informed about their commitment to the goals and purposes of the journey and fully participate in the journey process."

"Some journeys need a lot of planning. If people are going with you, use their strengths, too. This makes the journey a shared one and, for me, always richer. Other journeys are more 'go with the flow'" but in every case, I try to see what God is wanting, saying, prompting or in other ways influencing for his purpose."

I try to see what God is wanting, saying, prompting or in other ways influencing for his purpose.

Pacific participants thought of journeys as primarily cyclical. Some focused on the idea of repetition, others on return:

"Our journeys are always cyclical, except in death. There is always an expectation for return back to the village. Land is very important in our culture; it gives us our identity and sense of belonging. We cannot venture out to another place and not return to where we belong and what is ours."

"For sure cyclical. I guess a journey is a lifetime for me. What you face now you may face again, so how will you deal with it next time?"

"Cyclical when I am slow to learn something from a previous journey, like the children of Israel. If they are cyclical in that God is getting more recognition (glory) then cyclical is ok."

"Generally, cyclical – I set off from home and return home. However, on a longer trip where I am going to numerous destinations, I think of it as linear including returning home to end the trip. Hopefully, but not always, by thinking of it as linear, I can focus on one destination at a time rather than, 'when will I get home?'"

Prevalent themes in the responses of Pacific participants included purposefulness, journeying with others, and returning home. There was a noticeable solemnity to many Pacific responses and a primary focus on literal/physical journeys, often to find food and almost always traveling as a group. The responses from a number of the Pacific participants reflected flexibility, the importance of context, a holistic approach to preparation, and a sensitivity to people.

- The Pacific leader's statement, "It's not a journey if you don't leave", invites further reflection. What does it really mean to leave and what are you leaving? What are you willing to risk and what makes it a risk? What do you hope to gain?

Asia

Many Asian survey participants provided detailed explanations of how the concept of journey is communicated in their languages. Several expressed a variety of ways one can talk about journeys in Cantonese, sharing these characters for journey: 旅程 usually describes physical travel from one geographic location to another; 旅 means travelling; 程 means distance or progression. Another participant offered the same characters, saying they originally described "a unit of 500 soldiers, like a brigade". Soldiers were always on the move and were closely associated with the idea of journey. Other characters combined with each of these characters convey different journey emphases: 行程 (travel schedule), 歷程 (travel experience), 旅行 (travelling and walking), and 旅遊 (travelling and wandering). Relational aspects were also covered, with words for fellow sojourner, veteran sojourner, and "one who has gone on ahead".

Koreans borrow from the Chinese 旅程. The loan word in Korean for journey is 여정, *yeojeong*, meaning "the course of travel". It could also be "passage of life, process towards destination, or itinerary".

A Japanese leader shared that the Japanese character for *tabi* is the same as the Chinese character 旅. "There are numerous books, songs, tanka/haiku which talk about our life as one *tabi* (journey)." Another character, *michi*, 道 (also translated as "do"), expresses the idea of a journey to perfection. "Flower arrangement, calligraphy, judo, kendo, etc., are all perceived as a way to perfection. One never reaches perfection in this life, but pursuing perfection is very important." He related this to his life being on the journey toward perfection, following Jesus Christ.

From an Indonesian leader, "[I]n Bahasa we say *Perjalanan.*" The word indicates travelling a great distance and always traveling with others. (Bahasa Indonesia is the official language of Indonesia.)

An Indian participant said, "When we talk about a journey, we use the Sanskrit word *yaatra*, which describes a long trip, mostly to a distant place. This word is compounded with other nouns to make the purpose of the journey clear – pilgrimage, fun, mourning, etc."

An Indonesian leader said, "Leading my family on our spiritual journey (wife and two children): Each morning we start with the Lord, reading our Bible as a family and praying together. Each night we tell the God story for the children and kneel down together, praying to the Lord."

A Bangla speaker offered three words expressing different facets of journey. *Jatra* is traveling from one place to another, an outing. *Vroman* refers to a single travel experience or a series of journeys that have already been done, recently or in the past. *Shafour* refers to doing a tour that has a purpose, such as an educational tour.

One leader talked about several types of journeys:

> Journey for recreation – "[W]e reach the destination and we [are] all happy. Later happiness comes with the memories."
>
> Journey in harmony (love and relationship) – "[W]hen communities help each other and [are] willing to have an impact to live in harmony forever."
>
> Journey in spirituality – "[E]ach village/culture build[s] their strong commitment to worship God. Each year they celebrate the journey milestones and [are] willing to show to others."

From the Philippines, participants responded much like those in the Pacific group, relating journey to community. "Journey is *paglalakbay* in Tagalog. It is a meaningful word that includes family and/or friends." Also from the Philippines, "There is another word embedded in *paglalakbay*: *akbay*. It means to put an arm on a companion's shoulder." *Paglalakbay* is also associated with adventure and consideration of the future. "It is wondering how the future will look based on what I am now doing." Further Tagalog examples included:

> *Lakbay isip* (travel mind) – imagining the end goal of your journey.
>
> *Lakbay tanaw* (travel to review) – going back through the paths you've taken since you started the journey.

The Filipino custom of *bayanihan* is identified as a type of journey distinguished by communal unity, work, and cooperation toward a specific goal.

- These insights offer additional cultural connections and show distinctions between literal and metaphorical journeys, and between the various journeys we make in life and the journey that is life. How do these values resonate with missional intent? What examples do you see of the *bayanihan* qualities listed above?

One Asian leader described journey as a chance to learn and exposure to new things. There may be some anxiety beforehand but, once underway, there is excitement and adventure, fun, learning and growing, challenges, a new place, a new experience, and new friends. Others said that there had to be a purpose to the journey and that it could be taken alone or with others. If others were involved, they must want to achieve the same purpose, and there should be a leader. "It's about being together. Doing things together [...] sharing each other's joy, surprises, burdens."

> *It's about being together. Doing things together [...] sharing each other's joy, surprises, burdens.*

Almost all of the Asian participants said journeys were or could be both linear and cyclical. Notably, most drew distinctions as to when and why a journey could be considered linear and when it could be considered cyclical. "Chinese people believe where a person is born they should return. So, life is a journey back to its origins." One participant offered a perspective unlike those of the other participants. She said journey was neither linear nor cyclical. "I think of a journey as a spiral moving upward [...] even if it seems I am coming back to my point of origin, I am not the same 'me' anymore. I probably am on a higher ground. Given time and the experiences I gained, I change, hopefully becoming more mature and better."

People, purpose, and preparation were priorities for Asian leaders, as indicated in the following comments:

> **People** – Ask people with experience and learn from them. Make friends. Learn from locals. Bring gifts for renewing relationships. Bring people who have appropriate equipment and complementary skills. Who do you feel comfortable with, and who is like-minded in achieving the goal/objective of the journey? Put on cultural glasses to see the world. Have accountability partners. Choose people whose morals are rooted in the Word of God and really love God. Heed their rebuke and discipline as they speak out of love and concern. One leader noted that it was important to identify the people who travel with you because they are precious.

> **Purpose** – "Understanding the purpose and what is expected at the destination determines how I prepare." "There are journeys considered important for building relationships (for example, with in-laws), journeys to research new lands, journeys for economic reasons." Survey participants also mentioned milestones, goals, a sense of achievement, life as a journey, and lessons to be learned. "I unintentionally neglected the triune God in my life in the past and found out that's what's been missing all along in this journey I'm in."

> **Preparation** – Do the research, beware of pitfalls, decide how much time is required and what resources are required and available. Who can be resources themselves or provide those resources? Consider weather, health needs, insurance, money, visa, contingency plan. "Spiritual, physical, mental, and emotional preparations are needed. Pray, be rooted in the [W]ord, and be sensitive to the guidance of the Holy Spirit."

- How could the people, purpose, and preparation considerations above be applied to a review of your group or organisation's journey? If you made a list of these considerations, what else would you add to help you on your journey?

Africa

Personal and geographic context also significantly influenced how African survey participants described the concept of journey in their languages and cultures. In one African leader's primary language, the root of the word for journey is the word for walk, so "journey involves the idea of walking or movement, and distance". He also spoke with optimism about new discoveries and experiencing new cultures as a potential part of the journey.

One leader pictured journey as going from one town to another, having new experiences. His parents moved from town to town because of his father's job. The towns were mainly within the same cultural group, but there were always new experiences connected to making these journeys. Another told of growing up in a different cultural environment from his parents but being educated as he would have been in their home country. So, he grew up with the concept of journey as movement from a familiar zone to somewhere less familiar but with a strong emphasis on remembering where he came from.

One African leader mentioned his preference for travelling with others and the hope of returning home from a journey but also expressed his culture's acceptance of uncertainty. Another participant expressed the anticipation and excitement of new experiences but also acknowledged the unknown, the risk, and the possibility of either success or failure. She also spoke of excitement, anticipation, and the unexpected. In her language and culture, a journey meant travelling to one or more destinations and eventually returning home.

All of the African survey participants said a journey is cyclical and includes a return home. Those who acknowledged the possibility of the journey not being cyclical spoke of a linear journey as "denying your origin", or deciding to live elsewhere permanently. This makes a strong statement about their culturally-informed connection to home. However, there was one reference to the possibility of a journey being linear if that journey was our journey toward God. The participants also referred to journeys of acquisition, as mentioned earlier. Even if people leave home for a long time, there is an expectation that they will eventually come back with greater wealth or other resources.

Participants shared that the process of planning is to secure resources and ensure that the purpose of the journey can be achieved. For some journeys, you need to take everything with you; for others you can depend on available resources enroute. "Purpose will determine planning" was a recurring theme. "Take a tool with you (traditionally one should not start a journey without a stick and a knife – they are a survival kit); don't tire yourself carrying too much food or bedding, count on help along the way; but every man must carry his own sitting stool, you can't borrow one from a friend." Without cultural understanding, many who journey will fail to travel well.

One leader shared this beautiful and realistic picture of journeying together: "[I]f you want to go far, go with other people, but if there are no people to start the journey with, others will join you on the way, so be ready to accommodate new friends and sojourners with you; be ready that some of those who started the journey with you may not finish it with you – it's life."

- How can you learn and evaluate what's needed for your organisation's journey?
- Who has helped you along the way? How flexible are you in accommodating new or departing fellow sojourners?

Americas

The Spanish language, like many others, has more than one way to express the concept of journey. One respondent said, "I use the word *camino*, which literally means road, path." He explained that, in specific contexts, it is also understood as journey. "I can say, 'I know your *camino* has been full of challenges'."

Peregrinaje (pilgrimage) is another way to talk about journeys in Spanish. A Latin American participant stated that *peregrinaje* denotes action and relates to a trip, voyage, or travel. It is an opportunity to learn new things. Another said it also includes life experience beyond how one would talk about a vacation or work trip.

Other Spanish words for journey include *vida* (life) and *viaje* (trip). One leader commented, "We love to use metaphors, and for us, life is a trip, so we greet people saying '*como andas*' [How do you walk? How are you walking?]". He explained, "[A] journey is a trip made with other people. We 'walk' together sharing, […] understanding each other, helping others to succeed […]. A journey is an activity of life; it is life in itself." One leader explained that a *viaje* would be a short journey, whereas *camino* would express a long journey, perhaps a lifetime.

Another leader offered a broad description of journey, saying, "It is an experience that involves emotions, fatigue, joy, recharging batteries, […] responsibilities and burdens […] it is a story that has past, present and future […] experienced both in the dimension of the personal and community."

One survey participant contributed *jornada*, a Portuguese term for journey. He described it as follows: "A long process of maturing […]. Most journeys are [a] positive, life-changing collection of experiences that bring a person to a new unimaginable self."

"Always there is the strong component of 'return'," wrote a North American participant, referencing Tolkien's *The Hobbit* and the return home, but as a changed person. "It also includes the sense of adventure, some unknowns and some risk."

Most of the Americas survey participants saw journey as linear, although one said it was cyclical and several said it was both. The emphasis on a linear journey focused on change and growth. Several participants mentioned that even if you go home again, you are somehow new. One person mentioned an "unfolding", another spoke of terrains, emphasising that even a linear perspective is not a straight line. The participant who said that a journey was cyclical spoke of the need to return home or to your point of origin to share what has been learned or obtained with others. This responsibility and accountability factor is worthy of more exploration and connects to the issue of stewardship.

> *Even if you go home again, you are somehow new [...] even a linear perspective is not a straight line.*

Survey responses from the Americas often tied journey to both history and vision for the future. That, plus the sense of adventure often expressed, and an occasional streak of individualism, may reflect participants' national histories and stories of explorers, entrepreneurs, pilgrims, and immigrants.

There was also focus on beginnings and on outcomes:

> **Beginnings** – "It's necessary to understand the areas the Lord wishes to change in order to be open to begin the journey. Begin with prayer. Take much advice from those who share the same vision as well as taking them along with you together with those who are open to change."

> **Outcomes** – "I always think about the outcome. Once that is determined, many other aspects of the plan cascade. Planning to make the final scenario possible. Prayer, the plan, and outcome are in God's hands. Flexibility."

One Americas participant noted that "[it] depends on the type of journey – a literal physical journey or some other type of journey – as to how I plan, what I take, who comes with me, etc. If the destination is known, I think of what needs to happen to get there […]. My mind is busy, always thinking, listening and clarifying each step, listing what is needed, preparing or acquiring every item needed." Anyone accompanying is included in the process. "If it's a personal, spiritual, or emotional journey, though, it's a solitary journey." She also said that she includes others who seem "safe" and want to be a part of walking with her on the journey. Mostly family, maybe a close friend, but it can at times include a stranger. "I try to be open and listening, to see if there is anyone or anything needed in my journey that I might not have thought of as an obvious companion."

- How does looking at your history influence your thinking about the future?
- How do you decide whom to include? Who makes those decisions? Are there people you need to consider including who haven't been included?
- What part has prayer played in your planning?

Europe

A Danish leader reflected, "We have different words for journey which indicate the length, duration, and purpose of the journey as well as different words describing the means of transportation combined with the word for journey." She also talked about the spiritual journey or journey of life, and said, "There is a sense of growth, change and maturing tied to the concept of a spiritual journey which can be done alone or in fellowship."

A Norwegian leader said *reise* was the closest word to *journey* and could be either literal or metaphorical. It serves as both noun and verb or can mean "to travel". She stated, "It refers to movement of persons (usually), either in a physical sense, from one place to another, or it could refer to moving up the social ladder (*klassereise* – class journey), or changing viewpoints dramatically – political, religious or other [...]. We have a very much used noun denoting trip or journey, namely *tur*. It can be compounded in numerous ways, and is used a lot. It is perhaps more of a general term than 'journey' (*reise*) and can be used for anything like 'go for a walk' (*gå tur*), 'Sunday outing' (*søndagstur*), 'mountain hike' (*fjelltur*), 'boat trip' (*båttur*), 'road trip' (*biltur*), 'cabin trip' (*hyttetur*), just to give a few examples. Sometimes when you talk about travel, you can use *reise* and *tur* interchangeably." For this leader, the concept of journey had positive connotations and was associated with adventure, new experiences, growth, seeing/learning new things, new opportunities, and meeting new people.

German speakers also use the word *Reise*, as both literal and figurative. (Note: all nouns are capitalised in German.) One leader mentioned other travel-related words, including *Ausflug* (out-flight or outing, something you do to have a good time on the weekend or holiday with family or friends), *Trip*, *Expedition*, and *Exkursion*, all of which are similar in meaning to their English counterparts. There is also the phrase *Sich auf den Weg Machen* (to make oneself of the way). Usually used figuratively, it means to start and go on a way (or path). She elaborated on the concept of journey, saying it involves distance and leaving one's usual surroundings and routine. There will be both comfort and discomfort, leaving everyday responsibilities but also everyday routines. "All in all, a very positive feeling because it is something special [...]. [I]t also makes me think of new things and new experiences but also of rest, relaxation and just doing what I feel at the moment."

A Romanian participant connected exploration, adventure, and danger with the idea of journey. Memories from the era of communism in his country impacted his responses. In his earlier experience, journeys were either limited to holidays within the country or were more hazardous journeys to leave the country, possibly forever. This demonstrates how history, context, and personal experience shape each person's journey concept.

On a lighter note, an English participant claimed travel is now so easy and common, no one even talks about journeys much unless a trip is more involved or challenging than usual. Another British participant had a differing view and said it was common in their culture "for journeys to be considered difficult or boring, which is a reason to not undertake them". So, apparently, one group of Brits takes journeys and doesn't talk about them unless they have had harrowing experiences, which then discourages the other group from ever taking journeys at all.

A Slovakian leader saw the concept of journey as discovery, a possible solution to a situation. In Slovak, the word for journey also means way, but would not apply to a short trip. He said that the book *Pilgrim's Progress* is, in their language, *Pilgrim's Way*. Speaking of a journey, he said, "It will take time and I need to make an effort to reach my destination, it's not easy, requires significant involvement. It requires physical energy, preparation, transport, planning, and one should expect obstacles [...]. On my way [there may be] something new [...]. It is positive, and there is value to the journey." "Otherwise who would dare? [But it] may be tough before the sweet end. Prepare to sacrifice."

Excitement was expressed as well: "Interest in meeting new people, excitement to see new landscapes, and probably the most – learn new things and ideas, see new solutions/ideas/ways for my life. I always expect the journey will bring refreshment to my life and enlarge my horizon."

The majority of European participants said journey was linear, "[m]ostly because things can change while you are gone and a return journey may not be the same as the outward trip". Only one leader claimed it was cyclical rather than linear. Four said it was both. Again, there was an emphasis on the idea that, even if you return home, you are not the same.

Of all the regional leaders, the Europeans were most likely to refer to both metaphorical and literal journeys. "In the literal sense, most journeys bring you back home or to the starting point. Metaphorical journeys bring you to new 'homes', new situations or conditions that will be [the] starting point of the next phase."

European responses often referenced distinctions between preparing for a work trip or a vacation, a solo trip or a family trip. The participants' input often reflected personal preferences and experiences. One participant spoke specifically regarding organisational leadership. "For an organisation, it requires leaders who are open to new things, always wanting to develop, be flexible, adapt to new realities. No matter what kind of journey, it takes motivation and willingness to move (physically, emotionally, psychologically, spiritually)."

> *"No matter what kind of journey, it takes motivation and willingness to move (physically, emotionally, psychologically, spiritually)."*

We've seen the emphasis on flexibility, the assumption that journeys will include unknown factors. There are also frequent references to enthusiasm, optimism, and excitement.

- How could a journey mentality that includes this understanding make a difference in how you lead in your organisation or how you live your daily life? How would it change your expectations?

Other Observations

Survey Question 4 asked participants, "When you think of a journey, do you think of time, distance, or both, or something completely different?" The responses were as follows:

Time – 8; Distance – 6; Both – 33.

None of the Asian or American participants chose distance. None of the Africans chose time. The vast majority of participants from each region chose "both" but often with an "and" or "but" complement. They said the journey was about:

Experience – Including "depth of experience", "relational experiences given in the context of a long time". "It is the sense of newness or experience."

Out-of-the-box thinking – "Even if the journey is very personal, perhaps even unnoticed by others, I think of it as something that potentially can be revealed to others, something that (even without my knowing it) may add to their own journey." "A journey is an activity of life, it's life in itself."

Motivation – "These [time and distance] represent the how and what, but I think of the why. What is the purpose of the journey? What is our motivation?"

Practical concerns – Time, distance, seasons, cost, people, modes of transportation were all mentioned. For some, it was information needed to know the best place and time for hunting and fishing. For others, it was a more passive undertaking. At least one participant also included the importance of "food and a book".

Observations from Questions 7 and 12 are incorporated together into the section below.

Question 7: "What are some important aspects of a journey? How important is it to know the destination before you start?"

Question 12: "What other thoughts or concepts about the concept of 'journey' can you share?"

Common themes emerge as we read the participants' input on aspects of a journey. We can see the impact and influence of context. There is also the common experience of preparation and the every-journey necessities of planning and packing. And we hear that people, prayer, and holistic well-being are important factors in undertaking a journey, literal or figurative. Throughout all the questions and observations, it is also evident that purpose is considered essential to a journey.

Although we looked at much of the information according to regions of the world, most of the patterns stretch across geographic boundaries. However, the diversity of responses is enough to remind us that many factors affect perceptions. Individual personalities, cultural norms, national history, family background, and personal experiences all influence and shape perceptions.

Patterns of Perceptions

As we consider the emerging patterns and think of applying the journey concept to strategic thinking and planning around the world, its potential begins to take shape. Of the fifty-two leaders who participated in the survey, no one questioned the topic or seemed confused about the concept of journey. Their responses indicated a clear understanding of journey in the literal sense. Most participants also expressed ideas and thoughts regarding journey in the figurative sense. The majority expressed what could be considered a balanced impression of the concept of journey. Participants acknowledged that there were both positive and negative aspects. Excitement, anticipation, and new experiences were among the most commonly used descriptive words. Other commonly used words such as purpose, destination, preparation, change, transition, and return indicate serious intention and an understanding of the need to think and plan. There was also an acceptance of the realities of cost, obstacles, fatigue, setbacks, and difficulties.

There were four particularly notable themes in the survey responses: returning home, journeying together, the goal of acquisition, and focus on destination.

Returning home

For some survey participants, there was an assumption of, or a strong desire for, a journey to conclude with a return home. This often included the idea of being changed and/or having new experiences on the journey, or returning from the journey with something of value for one's family and/or community (see Acquisition section below). Among these participants, many expressed the return home as an essential element of the journey, as though a journey could not exist without it. Even when people couldn't return home, the desire to do so was often still there. From the participants' reflections and the insights we gained, we can consider how the idea of returning home does or doesn't fit with the concept of an organisation's journey of missional intent.

- It may be apparent where "home" is for physical journeys, but what and where is "home" when the journey is metaphorical?
- What are the possible implications for leaders when using the journey concept for strategy development? How can you create a sense of continuity (home) while also moving forward?

- What does your metaphorical home look like? Is it a place you plan to "return to", a place you leave behind, or a place (or ideal) you carry with you?

Journeying together

Journeying together was an assumption for some survey participants, and a desire or preference for others. There were also a few who preferred to journey alone or at least said it is simpler to travel alone. The diversity of responses makes sense when we look at context. One survey participant compared the ease of travelling alone on a business trip to planning a family vacation, and another expressed the necessity of fellow travellers when journeying to hunt or fish and provide for a community. There were numerous mentions of walking. Considering that many of the cultures represented do not consider walking as a primary means of transportation on a journey, it is meaningful that the image of walking together so often came to mind. Chapter 5 will help you think further about walking the journey. You may also want to reflect on the reality that mindsets will differ depending on whether you are from an individualistic or a collectivist culture. Personality may form the preference, but context usually makes the decision, and culture establishes the norms.

Valuing others, needing others, and sharing with others were among the ideas expressed in these participants' comments. Many other survey participants did not specifically mention journeying together or alone; some suggested that both were options, depending on the situation. But just as with the idea of returning home, some were emphatic about journeying together. Those leaders often seemed to have a clear picture of a specific type of journey. They knew why they were travelling and where they were going. They knew who would go with them.

- As a leader, how clear is your picture of journey for yourself and your organisation?
- How do you determine purpose, direction, and who goes with you?

Acquisition

Journeys are attempted for many reasons. One motivation, however, stood out among the responses: *acquisition*, the expectation of or commitment to learning something new or bringing something back. Whether the goal is a pig or a PhD, journeys are often made to obtain something – it may be food for the community, skills for one's livelihood, or the knowledge and joy obtained through new experiences. Some participants had very practical thoughts concerning gathering food or gaining new knowledge. However, many also revealed an enthusiasm that took the concept of journey past necessity to adventure.

Several participants referred to finding solutions. This is intriguing because it takes the journey concept beyond learning, growing, and acquiring new knowledge, to actually providing solutions. These solutions could theoretically be inspired by the knowledge gained, new things observed or heard, or they could even be found in new people met or in conversations held with various people along the way. The leaders offering these ideas didn't specify that they were trying to solve specific problems, indicating that the "solutions" acquired may lead to innovation and apply to situations and circumstances not even considered as "problems".

The acquisition theme presents many possibilities as we consider the journey concept, missional intent, and strategy. Several of the participants' comments revealed different twists on the acquisition theme. One emerging theme regards journeying together, then sharing what you learn with others who were not on the journey with you. Information "trickle down" is notoriously poor in many organisations. Further exploration of how to best share acquired knowledge or skills is certainly warranted.

- What do you seek and why?
- How can what you "acquire" (learn and discover) be applied?
- How can you, as a leader, share information, passion, vision, and purpose?

Destinations

As expected, destination was a common theme when reflecting on the concept of journey. For some, a journey is inconceivable without a clear destination in mind. For others, the destination provides motivation but doesn't have to be quite so specific. A number of participants acknowledged that paths and destinations could change as one proceeds on a journey. A few mentioned the idea of the process as more important than the destination, but far more linked the idea of destination with purpose. Almost all the survey participants made some mention of, and demonstrated that, they value purpose.

"The destination gives you hope and a sense of purpose. It helps you plan your steps."

"We will go together and reach the destination."

Expectations

The survey participants showed a high level of realism in their thinking. This is not surprising as they are all organisational leaders. Even though there was much enthusiasm and optimism regarding the journey, almost all participants expressed that a journey is not always easy, pleasant, or guaranteed to meet expectations. The leaders mentioned:

Responsibilities – Preparation, planning, packing, developing a team, building relationships, etc.

Resources – "Need for provision and equipment."

Stresses – "Sharing burdens" and sacrifice. "There is also a cost to consider." Physical and emotional cost, fatigue, need for rest, boredom, physical strain, pain, anxiety, apprehension, a long process of maturing, sadness, discouragement. "Sometimes there will be a feeling of disillusionment of ever being able to reach the next 'signpost'." Being out of one's comfort zone and "not having control".

Risk – "Difficulties, challenges, risk, and danger […] tough." "Could be dangerous (one might not return)." "Expect obstacles." "Fears of obstacles that will disrupt the journey."

People – "[M]uch depends on who your neighbour is in the train."

None of the survey participants expressed an escapist perspective or a romanticised view of what a journey might entail. When people come into the discussion as reflective practitioners with a realistic perspective based on experience and insight, there is less chance of false or overly idealistic hopes and expectations. Instead, there is far greater chance for understanding, agreement, and progress. Later chapters will look at challenges and common areas of focus, such as change and success, that can be impacted by journey thinking.

- What positive potential do you see in acknowledging difficulties, unknowns, the need for and inevitability of change? How could this help you assist your organisation and colleagues?
- What difference would it make if you approached your organisational strategies and planning from a journey perspective, complete with an acknowledgment of the ups and downs, the need for endurance, collaboration, ongoing learning, etc.? How would this differ from having a warfare, sports, or other competitive model that focuses on "winning"?

3. Journey Influences – Literature

> We are of the opinion that instead of letting books grow mouldy behind an iron grating, far from the vulgar gaze, it is better to let them wear out by being read.
>
> *Jules Verne, Journey to the Center of the Earth*

How might hobbits or a runaway egg influence your organisational journey and missional intent? Keep reading! Journey Survey Question 5 asked, "What ideas and stories from your culture/s are representative of the concept of a journey?" The results were less regionally focused than expected, showing the near-universality of many journey stories as well as the acceptance of the journey concept in general. Many participants' ideas and impressions of journey were shaped by internationally known literary classics, whether read for pleasure, studied at university, or heard at family story time. As children, we absorb stories and they become a part of our worldview. As adults, we add to and adjust that worldview depending on what else we hear and read.

As children, we absorb stories and they become a part of our worldview.

We will identify and examine some of the literature mentioned by survey participants and look at a sample of other literature, as well. As patterns emerge from the previous chapter and this chapter, we will be able to further explore the impact of journey stories on our own perceptions. As we encounter and identify types of journeys and journey themes, we will also be better able to recognise our own journey landscapes and discern journey principles applicable to ourselves and our organisations.

A Closer Look at Journey Literature

The prospect of danger, adventure, and discovery pulls us into journey stories. Journeys and quests are among the most common tropes in literature. This reflects and reinforces the idea that life itself is a journey. But, if being on a journey is our reality, why do we and our organisations often feel stuck, frozen in time, or incapable of figuring out in which direction to move next? Are we overly cautious, fearful, uncertain?

Even the wildest of journey tales can tell us something about ourselves and our possibilities. And they just might help us get unstuck and either ease us or unceremoniously dump us (in the tradition of great adventures) on the road to what's next. An online search will offer you dozens of lists of journey-themed books and their accompanying reviews. There's no shortage of resources. However, to get a global perspective, we will look at some of the authors and books mentioned by leaders who participated in the Journey Survey plus several that I've chosen. Our focus is on understanding influences which might help us comprehend how people perceive the concept of journey and help us connect the journey concept to missional intent, strategic thinking, and planning.

The Pilgrim's Progress

Several survey participants referenced *The Pilgrim's Progress*. A Bangladeshi leader mentioned its longstanding popularity in his culture. Bangla is one of the more than 200 languages into which the book has been translated. Published in 1678 and never out of print, John Bunyan's Christian allegory is considered the first English novel. Dickens, Twain, E.E. Cummings, C.S. Lewis, and Steinbeck all reference or pay homage to this journeying tale (Hofmeyr, 2004).

Professor of South African Literature Isabel Hofmeyr wrote an intriguing book exploring the history and influence of *The Pilgrim's Progress* in Africa. Bunyan's book, now translated into more than 80 African languages, was often illustrated with African drawings or dramatised photos and was widely adapted and embraced by the local cultures. Hofmeyr tells how African cultures made Christian's story their own. In England, Bunyan's book was later made "more British" by placing Christian, the main character, in an English landscape. Over the years, some wanted the book to be adaptable and international, some wanted to claim it for Britain as distinctly English literature, and others decried it as colonial and imperialist (Hofmeyr, 2004). The journey of *The Pilgrim's Progress* has continued far beyond what Bunyan imagined.

The translatability of the text, the universal nature of the message, and the appeal and ability to relate to the journey and those met along the way, have drawn people to this timeless tale. Worth more than just a single read, rereading the book at various times in life provides an opportunity to apply this allegory's wisdom to our context and journey.

The stories of Jules Verne

A Journey Survey participant with a penchant for time travel cited Jules Verne, C.S. Lewis, and Washington Irving's *Rip Van Winkle.* Another referred to Swift and Verne, saying, "We have stories like *Gulliver's Travels* [in German], and the Jules Verne books – *Journey to the Center of the Earth, Around the World in 80 Days*." French author Jules Verne understood the allure of a journey. In the fifty-four volumes of his series of *Voyages Extraordinaries*, he took readers around the world, to the moon and back, to the centre of the earth, deep into the sea, and on many other fantastic journeys.

Still considered one of the top five most translated authors in the world, Verne's most popular works have been translated into nearly 200 languages. His stories inspired youth and adults, including real-life scientists and explorers, some of whom made his stories come true. Verne was not, however, unreservedly pro-science. His early optimistic work gave way to later works that advised caution and consideration of other factors besides science and "progress".

It is no wonder several survey participants cited Verne. The wide availability of his stories and the appeal of their blend of science, history, exploration, and imagination captures the attention of a broad audience. Verne included the wonder, danger, adventure, challenges, and relationships that are a part of the journey. Reading Verne's books stirs the same excitement and anticipation expressed by many survey participants concerning the concept of journey. Although filled with fantastic events, these stories offer a picture of the possibilities and the responsibilities of journey leadership.

Peer Gynt

Before selfies, "me-time", and identity therapy, there was the grand narcissist, Peer Gynt. A Norwegian survey participant mentioned the book by her countryman, famed playwright Henrik Ibsen. *Peer Gynt*, written in 1867, is loosely based on an old Norwegian fairy tale. A mix of poetry and prose, surrealism and realism, the story moves through time and space to tell the story of Gynt, a selfish, lazy young man whose goal is to "be himself". Consumed by narcissism, he loses himself. Gynt makes one poor choice after another, be it with a troll king's daughter, as a businessman selling slaves and idols, as a prophet in the Middle East, or, ironically, being proclaimed Emperor of Self (a title he had long desired) by the inmates of an insane asylum. After much wandering, despair, and denial, he makes his way home. Gynt, now an old man, is confronted by a button moulder who has come to claim his soul to melt it down, as he is fit neither for heaven nor hell. Solveig, his true love who has waited all through the years, helps him see his true self (found only by not seeking self). Gynt asks, "Where was I as the one I should have been, whole and true, with the mark of God on my brow?" Solveig replies, "In my faith, in my hope, and in my love" (Ibsen, 2003: 235).

No matter how fantastical the story may be, Gynt, the wild seducer, egotist, and con man, is the everyman, a selfish sinner. The faithful and patient Solveig, whose name means "strong house" or "sun's path", represents redemption, salvation of the undeserving, a mirror of truth. Gynt's short-term companion Eberkopf's words ring true on the page and through the centuries: "But this same in-and-for-yourselfness, I'll answer for't, has cost you strife" (Ibsen, 2003: 108). Gynt's commitment to be true to his self only takes him further and further from who he was meant to be and all that could be his. This cautionary tale brings keen insights to the journey. It could have been written today, yet also resembles the proverbial warnings of King Solomon; it speaks to the prodigal, and has many philosophical and theological layers. Pride, lust, greed, knowledge, narcissism, power all play a part.

Gynt's dabblings in things religious are laughable until we consider our own less humorous compromises and failings. "And, as one needs in days of trial some certainty to place one's trust in, I took to religion intermittently. That way it goes more smoothly down. One should not read to swallow all, but rather see what one has use for" (Ibsen, 2003: 110). Peer Gynt was not the first nor the last to choose selective application and interpretation of Scripture. Convinced he could not give up his sinful ways of importing idols, he tried to "neutralise" his evil with good. "To stop the trade with China was impossible. A plan I hit on – opened straightway a new trade with the self-same land. I shipped off idols every spring, each autumn sent forth missionaries, supplying them with all they needed, as stockings, Bibles, rum, and rice" (Ibsen, 2003:112). Many try this same sort of bargaining every day, if not on such a global scale.

Gynt's journey takes him across the world, and his choices and circumstances often run him aground. Through it all, he seeks to be true to his "Gyntish Self" until he comes face-to-face with himself as he peels an onion, stripping layer after layer away, reaching not a core but nothing. There is no time here to go into the lessons of each leg of his journey, but they are many. Gynt's journey brings him back home, but not with the fanfare and riches he once dreamed of. There is the round-trip journey and the acquisition, perhaps, of his true self, recognising his wretchedness and reaching out to accept his redemption.

There is the round-trip journey and the acquisition, perhaps, of his true self, recognising his wretchedness and reaching out to accept his redemption.

J.R.R. Tolkien and C.S. Lewis

Not surprisingly, Tolkien and Lewis were among the authors mentioned by survey participants. Much is written elsewhere about these authors, their stories, and their influence. So here, again, we will focus on how their depictions of journeys might influence readers' perceptions of journey. Primarily through quotes from a few of their well-known works, we will look at several themes they have in common:

- beginnings (choosing those who take the journey);
- practical considerations for a journey;
- hazards and highlights of the journeys;
- lessons learned along the way;
- endings.

Beginnings – extraordinary journeys and ordinary people

What can we learn from the authors' descriptions of the travellers as they were chosen for and began their journeys? These characters all became leaders. What do they teach us about leadership?

Tolkien describes hobbits as "[L]ittle people, about half our height, smaller than the bearded dwarves. Hobbits have no beards. There is little or no magic about them […] they are inclined to be fat in the stomach" (1966: 16).

Bilbo first declined Gandalf's invitation to adventure and often had misgivings as he went on his "burglaring" journey. "Bother burgling and everything to do with it. I wish I was at home in my nice hole by the fire, with the kettle just beginning to sing" (Tolkien, 1966: 43).

Gandalf's words to Frodo: "You may be sure that it was not for any merit that others do not possess: not power and wisdom, at any rate. But you have been chosen, and you must therefore use such strength and heart and wits as you have" (Tolkien, 2002: 61).

Lewis describes his equally unlikely Narnia adventurers. In *The Lion, the Witch, and the Wardrobe* (1994), four children, Peter, Lucy, Susan, and Edmund, are sent away from war-ravaged London to stay with an uncle in the countryside. *The Voyage of the Dawn Treader* (1970) introduces Eustace Clarence Scrubb, a "puny" (1970f:2) bullying boy (soon to be reformed). In *The Silver Chair* (1970e), there is Jill Pole, in tears when we first meet her, a victim of school bullying. *The Horse and His Boy* (1970c) introduces us to the downtrodden boy Shasta found in a poor fishing village, mistreated by his assumed father … who is trying to sell him.

Other Narnia travellers are the first to admit their shortcomings. Horse (Fledge) to Aslan: "I don't know why it should be me – I'm not a very clever horse" (Lewis, 1970a: 144). Caspian to Aslan: "'I was wishing that I came of a more honourable lineage.' 'You come of the Lord Adam and the Lady Eve,' said Aslan. 'And that is both honour enough to erect the head of the poorest beggar, and shame enough to bow the shoulders of the greatest emperor on earth. Be content'" (Lewis, 1970b: 211).

These characters come from humble beginnings and demonstrate even more humbling behaviours and actions along the way. Yet these characters are chosen. We find them endearing. We cry and rejoice with them. We cringe and cower with them … because they are us. And like some of them, we, too, have discovered that we are children of the King.

Practical considerations

How were these characters equipped for their journey?

"'All the same,' said Susan presently, 'I suppose we'll have to make some plans. We shall want something to eat before long.' […] 'We've got the sandwiches Mother gave us for the journey,' said Edmund" (Lewis, 1970b: 4).

"Then Tirian gave Jill a bow and a quiver full of arrows. The next business was to light a fire […]. Dinner was, however, a dull meal […]. 'I wish we'd brought a packet of tea,' said Jill. 'Or a tin of cocoa,' said Eustace" (Lewis, 1970d: 55).

Dwalin to Bilbo: "You will have to manage without pocket-handkerchiefs, and a good many other things, before you get to the journey's end. As for a hat, I have got a spare hood and cloak in my luggage" (Tolkien, 1966: 42).

"'Nine o'clock we'd call it in the Shire,' said Pippin aloud to himself. 'Just the time for a nice breakfast by the open window in the sunshine. And how I should like breakfast. Do these people ever have it, or is it over? And when do they have dinner, and where?'" (Tolkien, 2002: 760).

For all who travel to new places, unless on a cruise ship with endless buffets, Pippin's questions regarding food will sound familiar. The practical considerations of both Lewis' and Tolkien's travellers are pretty basic – food, water, clothing, a few weapons for defence, a little mending, making do, and magic/help from time to time. These, plus obtaining directions and learning about the locals and the lay of the land, are primary concerns when on a journey. Travellers' basic needs remain the same even in the face of new worlds and grand adventures.

These humble hobbits, horses, and schoolchildren are not well-trained or prepared for what's ahead; many are barely coping with life. They have flaws; they complain; they get tired and hungry. In the case of the hobbits, they get hungry quite often. They are very much like us. And yet, they are chosen to undertake extraordinary journeys, experience remarkable events, meet unimagined creatures, dangers, challenges, wonders. They are tasked with goals they didn't even know existed in places and times they'd never imagined. In many ways, they remain conspicuously ordinary throughout their extraordinary journeys. However, as they learn to both follow and lead, they become part of something much bigger than themselves.

Hazards and highlights

Frodo recalls Bilbo's words: "'It's a dangerous business, Frodo, going out your door,' he used to say. 'You step onto the road, and if you don't keep your feet, there's no knowing where you might be swept off to'" (Tolkien, 2002: 73).

From Gandalf's letter: "Not all those who wander are lost" (Tolkien, 2002: 170).

Gimli to Elrond: "Faithless is he that says farewell when the road darkens" (Tolkien, 2002: 280).

Haldir to Merry: "The world is indeed full of peril, and in it there are many dark places; but still there is much that is fair, and though in all lands love is now mingled with grief, it grows perhaps the greater" (Tolkien, 2002: 348).

"Peter did not feel very brave; indeed, he felt he was going to be sick. But that made no difference to what he had to do" (Lewis, 1994: 144).

Susan to her siblings: "Let us go on and take the adventure that shall fall to us' (Lewis 1994:204).

"And here he was, a little halfling from the Shire, a simple hobbit of the quiet countryside, expected to find a way where the great ones could not go, or dared not go" (Tolkien, 2002: 644).

Lewis' and Tolkien's characters, although sometimes up for a bit of adventure, are not usually seasoned travellers. In some cases, they are reluctant travellers. More often than not, they are taken by surprise when they discover what is expected of them. They are even more surprised to learn that, with some help, they can be and do more than they thought possible.

> *They are even more surprised to learn that, with some help, they can be and do more than they thought possible.*

The stories have a common theme of journeying and discerning together, learning who and what to trust, and learning what is and is not important.

Lessons learned

"'Short cuts make for delays,' argued Pippin" (Tolkien, 2002: 88). To which Frodo replied, "Short cuts make delays, but inns make longer ones" (Tolkien, 2002: 88).

Gandalf: "Pity? It was Pity that stayed his [Bilbo's] hand. Pity, and Mercy: not to strike without need." A bit further in the conversation, Frodo cries out, "He [Gollum] deserves death." Gandalf replies, "My heart tells me that he has some part to play yet, for good or ill, before the end; and when that comes, the pity of Bilbo may rule the fate of many – yours not least" (Tolkien, 2002: 59).

"What you see and hear depends a good deal on where you are standing: it also depends on what sort of person you are" (Lewis, 1970a: 125).

"The further up and the further in you go, the bigger everything gets, the inside is larger than the outside" (Lewis, 1970d: 180). Mr. Tumnus uses the image of an onion. You may recall the shrinking onion of Peer Gynt's life, but in this case, having arrived at eternity's door, the onion grows larger, not smaller, as each layer is peeled.

Most of the lessons we learn along with these characters aren't spelled out. They are demonstrated in the characters' actions and attitudes as they grow in understanding, compassion, and wisdom along the journey. And they become our opportunity to grow as well.

Endings

The hobbits sing Bilbo's walking song:

Home is behind, the world ahead,
And there are many paths to tread.
Through shadows to the edge of night,

Until the stars are all alight.
Then world behind and home ahead,
We'll wander back and home to bed.
(Tolkien, 2002: 77)

Bilbo to Frodo: "I am sorry. I am sorry you have come in for this burden; sorry about everything. Don't adventures ever have an end? I suppose not. Someone else always has to carry on the story. It can't be helped" (Tolkien, 2002: 232).

Aslan to Peter, Lucy, and Edmund: "The term is over: the holidays have begun. The dream is ended: this is the morning" (Lewis, 1970d: 183).

In each story and for each journey, there is a sense of an ending. Some endings come with relief, most with a tinge of sadness at the parting of ways, the adventure letdown – when one goes back to ordinary life … if there is such a life. Some endings come with the sense of a job well done, a catastrophe averted, a problem solved. There's been growth, character-building, new friends made, and enemies subdued … for the moment. But the stories also hold the promise that the journey never really ends. It may look different in the future, it may happen in another place or time, perhaps even with different companions. For some, the journey is a round-trip, back to the safety of home. For others, it leads to an unexpected new home. And for still others, the journey has just begun.

- What hazards are you facing on your journey? Which were expected? Which weren't?
- The learning of lessons never ends. What lessons have you learned along your journey? How have you shared them? Who has helped you through sharing their journey learnings?
- Where are you in your journey? What might the end look like? How will you finish well?
- Where is your organisation on its journey? Do you see the potential for an end of your organisation as you know it? Is that ending seen as a positive or a negative? What might an ending look like, and what might the circumstances of that ending be? How do you see your organisation continuing if you don't imagine an end? What can you imagine it becoming?

Folk and Fairy Tales

Lewis and Tolkien drew their stories from their vivid imaginations and their great wealth of knowledge of folk and fairy tales, mythology, and history. Thousands of earlier authors wrote stories that flowed, changed course, merged, and fed into this sea of journey literature. Many folk and fairy tales feature adventurous travel and teach profound lessons. Stories like those about the Bremen Town Musicians and *Das Tapfere Schnederlien* (The Brave Little

Tailor) feature heroes who travel, often because of a lack of funds, luck, or family, to find their fortunes.

In answer to the Journey Survey, a Slovakian leader told the tale of an egg that goes on a journey. The egg meets and collects a group of elderly animals one by one. For all their individual weaknesses, as a group they succeed. They reach shelter, which happens to be a robbers' hideout. But the travellers hide, scare the robbers, and eventually have a peaceful night of safe shelter. Even without hearing the story in full, we can identify several key journey themes, including travelling better together, young and old together, overcoming dangers and hurdles, and a successful arrival. Like the story of the egg, which resembles the perhaps better known story of *The Musicians of Brementown* (Grimm & Grimm, n.d.), many stories are similar from country to country, but the characters, details, and settings may change.

The Slovakian leader went on to mention the folk and fairy tales of young men who go on a journey to learn something, return, and succeed because of their new knowledge or skills. You can probably recall stories of sons who return with money, a princess, a treasure, a trade. Many of these stories reflect the times in which they were created. In poor areas with few jobs, people travelled to find itinerant work: repairing household items, harvesting, building, logging. They learned new things and saw new sights, often bringing their stories and trades back home. Other stories tell of bedraggled soldiers on their way home from war and how they find (and sometimes lose) their fortune. These stories are found in countries around the world.

Another survey participant shared some of the many Filipino stories or *alamat* (a Bikol and Tagalog word for legend, folklore, or story) about journeys. One such story, *Ibong Adarna* (Adarna Bird), is about the journey of three brothers looking for a particular bird that can cure their father. The story shows how the younger brother's patience and self-sacrifice save the father and the two older brothers.

To look a little deeper, I chose four books of classic fairy tales from my own library and approximately a dozen stories found online to broaden the global scope (Grimm & Grimm, 2014; Anon, 1936; Anon, 1945; Beaumont, 1756; Stern, 1946; Fairytalez.com). Don't let the "fairy tale" category deter you from engaging with these stories. These stories of adventure, risk, and daring are a treasure house of metaphors and multiple levels of meaning. To learn more, I chose stories in which a journey and events on that journey play vital roles. I then looked for patterns, finding three main types of journeys. Finally, I noted other similarities.

Types of journey

Nearly half of the approximately one hundred fairy tales reviewed involve a significant journey. Most include persons (usually young men) who leave home to make their fortune, find a princess, or learn new skills. If the story is about one young man, he usually returns home victorious after learning life lessons, encountering dangers, and becoming generally more worldly-wise. Not all end with a happily-ever-after, however. Sometimes, the main character has been foolish, unlucky, or deceived and returns home in the same or worse state than before. Some characters begin foolish and end foolish. Some grow wiser.

About a fifth of the stories featured three brothers. "Once there were three brothers from the region of the Black Mountains. Originally they were very poor and travelled to Spain" (Grimm & Grimm, 2014: 126). So begins one example, *The Tablecloth, the Knapsack, the Cannon Hat and the Horn*. In this and many other such stories, the two older brothers are usually rude and greedy, but the underdog, the polite and kind younger brother, gets the girl and the happy ending. These stories, happily-ended or otherwise, usually fit into the round-trip category.

The one-way stories are a second type. They usually start similarly to the round-trip stories but end with the main character (usually a man, but occasionally a woman) remaining in the king's palace or whichever new location provided a happily-ever-after of riches and/or a spouse. "His subjects received him with joy; he married Beauty, and lived with her many years; and their happiness, as it was founded on virtue, was complete" (Beaumont, 1756: 14). Much of the story has changed through the years, but Beauty still ends up in the castle with her prince.

Flight stories are another common type. An evil stepmother, extreme poverty, a bullying big brother, or a free-loading ogre, force the innocent but wily main character to flee for their life. Adventures and colourful characters are encountered on the journey. The main characters often pick up new friends who, in the end, help them obtain riches or at least a roof over their heads. Notably, the flight stories are the ones that most often have an ensemble cast rather than an individual hero. Such is the earlier mentioned Slovakian story of the Egg and the Grimm Brothers' *Musicians of Brementown*. "After this the robbers never again dared enter the house. But it suited the four musicians of Bremen so well that they did not care to leave it any more" (Grimm & Grimm, n.d.).

There is another popular type of journey story that does not tidily fit any of the three categories described so far. Most of these stories feature a soldier, young or old, released from the king's army after a war. Sometimes, the soldier was promised good pay but did not receive it. In other cases, the lack of funds is just part of life. The soldier is often heading in the general direction of home. However, many of these soldiers have nothing and no one left at home. "The Soldier served God and the Great Tzar for twenty-five years, earned his three dry biscuits, and set off to walk his way home" is the beginning of "The Soldier and Death" from Arthur Ransome's collection of retold Russian tales (Ransome, 1922: 7). These soldier stories somehow seem the most true to life. Destitute elderly peasants (also common in many non-journeying stories) and wandering soldiers make the fairy tale landscape – be it Russian, Chinese, or Arabian – suddenly seem real.

Sooner or later, the soldiers make their way home, find a new stopping place, or die. Without creating a fourth category of journey on their behalf, we do need to recognise the significance of a wandering phase that can take place in any journey. This also includes the potential of losing one's way, of being lost. In fairy tales and in real life, we don't always learn the end of the story or the journey. Some of our wandering soldiers accumulate wealth through creative means and return home heroes. Others take jobs as gardeners. And still others… well, we just don't know their fate. In the story above, the soldier cheats Death and is turned away from both Paradise and hell, so "may be living yet" (Ransome, 1922: 46).

> *In fairy tales and in real life, we don't always learn the end of the story or the journey.*

Thus far we have explored many journeys, both literal and figurative, with Journey Survey participants, in personal lives and in literature. Among the many patterns that could emerge, there seem to be three distinct types of journey. They are identified here as follows:

- Round-trip – coming home – what will you bring back?
- One-way – a new destination – where will you go?
- Flight – leaving is the goal – how will you survive?

As we look at journey influences and the concept of journey, we can also keep these three types of journeys in mind..

- How can the types of journeys and their distinctions be helpful as you look at your organisation? Can you think of an example of situations or times when one of these types of journey represents your experience?
- Perhaps you can identify each of these types of journey as different legs of your journey, personal or organisational. How did you respond?

Themes and Types

Journey Survey participants citing literature sometimes mentioned books from their own culture, but more often went further afield. This was not unexpected, particularly given the participants' global interests, life experiences, and the fact that so many international classics are journey stories. As we identify patterns and themes in literature and in Journey Survey responses, there are many possibilities for consideration. Two topics in particular grabbed my attention as I looked for insights into applying the journey concept for determining missional intent, strategic thinking, and planning. The first topic focuses on journeying themes. I identified four, as noted in the previous chapter: returning home, journeying together, acquisition, and the importance of destination. The second topic explores types of journeys: round-trip, one-way, and flight, as noted above.

There is no direct correlation between the themes and journey types, but there are connections. Most obviously, the theme of "returning home" relates to the round-trip journey. There may be variances, however, when "home" means ancestral home rather than one's own home. But, for the most part, as exemplified in Journey Survey participants' comments, returning home is part of the round-trip journey. As one participant stated, "A journey includes a return home, but changed [...] always there is a strong component of 'return'."

"Journeying together" can be seen in examples of any of the three types of journeys. For all the legends of heroes, explorers, and pioneers who theoretically journeyed alone, very few actually did. Even the most "rugged individualists" usually had travelling companions, or at least a support team behind them. The literature mentioned in this chapter speaks to the commonality of travelling companions.

The theme of "acquisition" is closely tied to the round-trip journey. The entire purpose of a round-trip journey is often to acquire something, be it knowledge, wealth, food, or other goods, or to bring a friend, family member, or future spouse back home. In chapter 2, a Pacific leader spoke of "bringing back meat and food for the family or community". Acquisition can also be a goal of a one-way or flight journey. The acquisition could be a better life, home, or new discoveries. A European leader spoke of the many people who, in times past, left his country "for a better life or workplace". History is full of stories of immigrants who made long journeys to acquire new lives for themselves and their families. Some left by choice; others fled homelands which had turned hostile, or countryside which had become barren and infertile.

The theme of "the importance of destination" displays itself differently in each type of journey. On a round-trip journey, the outbound destination is usually known. Survey participants spoke of the destination as providing a sense of purpose for the journey. Whether going to the shore to fish or to a friend's home to visit, there is a destination, aim, purpose, endpoint. This is the "there and back again" journey in Tolkien's *The Hobbit* (1966), a journey that depicts all four themes. On a one-way journey, the destination may be known or unknown, depending on if one has a specific destination in mind or if one is journeying in search of something that will then determine the destination (a new place to live, a source of water, available land, agreeable climate, etc.). The same would hold true for a journey of flight. A person might flee danger or ruin without knowing the final destination, or might flee with a set destination in mind.

Returning home. Journeying together. Acquisition. The importance of destination. Each of these themes can play an essential role in discussions of and decisions concerning missional intent, strategic thinking, and planning.

- What are leaders' and followers' expectations and priorities regarding these themes? How could they be applied to help increase organisational communication and motivation?
- How could you apply the theme of returning home to topics such as core values, mission, vision?

- How could you use the theme of journeying together to create community or resolve conflict?
- How might a healthy round of discussions on acquisition goals and expectations clarify true priorities and lead to a healthier organisation?

Leading a team to appreciate and make the most of the journey as an essential part of reaching the destination could bring greater focus and contentment. These are just a few ways that reflecting on these themes can enrich an organisation.

The story continues.

4. Journey in History

History is a guide to navigation in perilous times. History is who we are and why we are the way we are.

David McCullough, address at Wesleyan University

History shapes the journey. The journey shapes history. The stories that emerge shape the generations to come.

Journey stories from history can be as fantastical as a fairytale or as down-to-earth as a dusty trail. They have a significant impact on our perception of journey. We can learn much about the world and life, not only through our journeys, but also the journeys of others, including those who lived long ago. Recognising our diversity of experiences and history also helps us know how to relate to others on the journey and helps us not be as surprised when others don't react in the same ways that we do.

> *We can learn much about the world and life, not only through our journeys, but also the journeys of others.*

Journey Survey Question 6 asked, "What historical events represent the concept of a journey in your history and culture/s?" Survey participants provided a wide range of examples, mentioning events and personalities. Here we share a sampling of responses, organised by geographic regions to highlight similarities among nations with some shared or comparable history. We will also look at three historical journeys in greater depth to discover more about our own journeys.

Europe

Nordic

Not surprisingly, Vikings were a common reference for participants from Denmark, Norway, and Sweden. Centuries ago, these nations were Viking kingdoms ruled by minor kings. The Vikings travelled extensively for trade, exploration, and expansion. To "go Viking" still means to travel abroad by sea (now minus the raiding).

"The story of our forefathers, the Vikings, building boats and sailing to different parts of mainly Europe is still present in today's [Danish] society in terms of symbols and names (very few follow the old religion of the Vikings). We tend to forget the brutality of their actions and instead praise them for their courage and ability to take action."

A Norwegian leader cited Viking Leif Erikson's journey to America centuries before the Spanish/Portuguese and they also spoke of Arctic explorers who are central to Norwegian cultural identity, heritage, and history. "Norwegian explorer Roald Amundsen was the first person on the South Pole and possibly (disputed) on the North Pole. There have been famous expeditions crossing Greenland by skis. Norwegians take great pride in these accomplishments, and the explorers are seen as national heroes."

A Swedish leader showed less reserve as he told of the sailing, pillaging, stealing, and trading of their Viking forebearers. He also cited Saint Birgitta's arduous pilgrimage to Jerusalem in the 1300s, and King Gustav Vasa's daring escape from Danish soldiers, skiing through the forests of Dalarna (central Sweden) in the 1400s. A more recent epic was that of the million Swedish people who moved to the USA in the 1800s. Population growth, crop failure, and religious and political persecution in Sweden resulted in many Swedish people leaving their homeland.

Central/Eastern Europe

The Polish people have a long history of travel. However, as one leader pointed out, the contexts and reasons differ significantly from past to present. In the past, political and economic turmoil forced people from their homes in desperation. Now, they go and return by choice as professionals, students, or tourists.

Another leader recalled, "During [the] communist time our travel was short, within the country [Romania], visiting the beautiful mountains or the sea. A few managed to travel abroad, leaving family behind, usually not coming back." After communism's 1989 collapse, many people travelled to Central and Western Europe for a better life or workplace, still often having to leave family behind. Even after the fall of communism, travel wasn't safe, and it was difficult to return home. Later, when Romania became part of the European Union, many more Romanians began travelling.

A Russian leader referred back to the 1600–1700s when Tsar Peter the First travelled the world and brought back new ideas which broke down barriers and encouraged development in his long-isolated country. Historian Michael Simmons wrote, "When Peter came into his maturity, his fascination with the society, technologies, and military traditions of Europe would lead him on a journey west; when he returned to Russia, it was at the head of a cultural revolution" (2016: 30).

More from Europe

From England, a leader with a different perspective: "Our culture doesn't have very many stories about journeys – they are all about destinations. We have a history of settlers and explorers going to other parts of the world. Their stories focus on the challenges of being in a new place, more than on the journey itself." He shared an anecdote, saying that the first English settlers in Australia planted crops according to the northern hemisphere timeline. "Obviously [they] hadn't learned much on the journey," he quipped.

A German leader shared the concept of *Wandern*, walking or hiking. This concept also relates to the centuries-old tradition of the *Zimmermann* (carpenter/builder), who travels across Europe for three years after his apprenticeship to finish his training. *Journeyman* would be another translation for this role. It is notable that the concept and practice of journeymen still exists and takes different but related forms in many places around the world.

Unlike most participants, the Swiss leader didn't see journeys as a significant part of their history. "Maybe trips over the mountains, alps? But maybe Swiss people are so stable regarding location in the past that we don't have such stories?" Intrigued by this historical stability, a bit of research unearthed the fact that in the eighteenth century, when many other Europeans were on the move, the Swiss considered emigration a crime "equivalent to desertion" (Faust, 1920: 5). Although there was emigration, particularly to the USA, in those years, the Swiss government made it a challenging process.

- The story of the English in Australia is a good reminder that what worked in the past won't necessarily work in the future. Can you think of an example in your context? What new knowledge have you gained on your journey? How have you applied it?
- Many of the stories are about going to a new place, willingly or out of necessity. What challenges have you and your team or group faced in a "new place" (literal or figurative)?

Africa

African participants shared that much of their history involved difficult journeys for the sake of survival or a better life. One leader cited "migrations in search of food and better cultivation land". Another explained, "Some of our cultures celebrate and commemorate the journeys they undertook from their ancestral home to their current location. Festivals are even organised to mark this. It becomes a historical landmark among the people."

One leader wrote a more extensive story about the migration of his people (highlighted later in this chapter). He said this history includes "the migration of my ethnic group to its present geographic location, the conflicts of encounters with different ethnic groups in that migration, and the hand of the supernatural that led the migrants".

- Hardships, difficult choices, and conflict are common to many journeys. How have you commemorated such journeys in your life or organisation? What is the value of acknowledging these milestones?
- How can you journey well when you don't know your destination? How do you lead such a journey? How can a leader determine when to move, when to stay?

Asia

Asia's long, documented history offers many examples of journeys, including those of explorers, refugees, people deeply attached to their land, and those without land.

One leader stated, "My people are called the Hakka, the 'guest people', because we migrated from the north and settled where we were welcome. For them, it was about survival and necessity as their ancestors migrated to seek a better future." The Chinese diaspora, through the centuries, dramatically portrayed an intense desire for a better future for their family. The perilous journey was preferred to the status quo.

From a leader in Hong Kong we learn, "I think of an example – the imperial examination. In Imperial China, there were civil service examinations to select male candidates for the state bureaucracy." The exams were regarded as a ladder for "climbing up" to a higher social status and a prosperous future. Candidates had to study hard beforehand, save a sum of money, and then travel from their homes to Beijing, the capital city. The journey could take a month or two, depending on their starting point and means of transportation. The fastest and easiest means were by carriage or horse. However, because of cost, most candidates travelled on foot. He commented, "Taking the imperial examination in ancient China was a journey full of challenges. Yet, many Chinese men still took it as an opportunity to a brighter future. We have many fairy tales related to this system." These are classic stories of quests, examples of perseverance and persistence.

Singaporeans focused on the relatively recent founding of their nation and its journey from swamp to significance. One leader said, "As a Singaporean, the inauspicious beginning as an independent country in Aug 1965 [was a] first step of a long journey to become one nation and also thrive as one people." He recalled how the three to four major ethnic groups that established the country had little in common besides the fact that each group represented hundreds and thousands of years of history. "Only on looking back do we see the contours of our journey as a disparate community."

Another leader reflected on the Singaporean journey. "The journey [...] began with the passion of one man, our former prime minister. Mr Lee Kuan Yew (LKY) [who] with his friends with similar passion and vision fought for the independence of Singapore." LKY developed Singapore into the diverse, modern metropolis it is today, but there were many sacrifices along the way. "[Now] LKY has to rely on his successors to continue to preserve this harmonious state in Singapore to continue to build on the foundation laid down by him and his comrades in the past." Singaporeans know their story and find purpose in their history. They understand what it took to bring them to where they are today as a nation and as diverse, yet unified, people.

A Korean leader shared, "[I] think modern Korean history represents it [the journey] quite dramatically. As soon as the Chosun Dynasty ended in the late 19th C[entury], Korea suffered under Japanese Occupation from 1905–1945. Ever since the liberation, there have been incessant political turbulences." He went on to mention the establishment of the Korean government in 1948, the Korean War 1950–1953, the "volatile and corrupt regimes" up until the early 1960s, followed by autocratic military governments until the late 1980s, and then democratisation through much bloodshed, and finally, the current government. "What a journey!" he exclaimed in closing.

Sharing a powerful story of historical relationship, an Indonesian leader commented, "In Maluku, we have a cultural tradition called *Pela*. *Pela* means two or more villages commit together to a journey of love for each other. Mostly *Pela* happens between Muslim and Christian villages, but sometimes Christian and Christian or Muslim and Muslim." When villages commit to *Pela*, this means that they will maintain a loving relationship.

From the Philippines, a leader wrote of the Bataan Death March in April of 1942 when, during the early years of World War II, 76,000 prisoners (66,000 Filipinos, 10,000 Americans) were forced to march 66 miles (106 km). Many died on the march, and many more died later in the prison camp.

From India, a leader noted the commonalities in much of world history. The arrival of foreign troops, war, conquest – "everything begins with a journey, people moving across nations, seeking new territories and trade. This is precisely the history of India also." Other types of journeys included those searching for spiritual enlightenment and propagation of religion. This Indian leader referenced the history of Christianity in her home state, starting with the journey of Saint Thomas in the first century A.D.

A leader from Bangladesh noted that most religions in Bangladesh have rituals or festivals related to journeys. He also saw their many periods of war as similar to journeys, citing their nine months of liberation war in 1971. And he recalled numerous historical and cultural influences on the perception of journey. He commented that Christians understand that this life is a pilgrim's journey.

- The realisation that status quo is not enough can be the beginning of a new phase of a journey or a new journey altogether. What are some motivating factors that keep your organisation or team moving forward?
- Where is the passion in your organisation or on your team? What is your passion? How has passion shaped your organisation?
- Where have you seen the need for perseverance? For sacrifice? How have you seen leaders lead well in these situations?

Pacific

In Papua New Guinea (PNG), a leader mentioned the Kula Ring, "a journey that involves trading, building relationships and friendships amongst people of various islands in the Milne Bay Province. My father comes from one of these islands. It involves deep cultural trading of valuable shells and necklaces, and relationship building amongst other things."

Another leader from PNG said, "My parents were in the first generation that witnessed the arrival of the (Methodist) missionaries (from Australia, New Zealand, and the South Sea Islanders from Fiji, Samoa, Tonga, Rarotonga). They [my parents] too, had their journey 'from darkness to light'." The journey of the gospel progressed quickly from there, one generation to the next. This leader has served more than thirty years with PNG BTA (an organisation within the Wycliffe Global Alliance, serving in Bible translation in PNG).

From New Zealand, "Our Pacific and Māori cultures are very family and relationship orientated […]. [T]his is very healthy given the influence our country gets from other more western cultures with a huge emphasis on the individual and now bureaucracy." This leader continued to talk about their tradition of starting relationships and journeys together with a handshake, not legislation. "So, I find I like to retreat more and more into close natural friendships with my Pacific brothers to experience deeper family journeys."

Writing about Samoa, a leader said, "Our ancestors were navigators, that's how we got to our island. They understood the signs of the seasons and time as well as land and sea. And, when we believed in the Good News, we were the ones who took the gospel to the other Pacific islands."

- How do you, as a leader, develop relationships and friendships? Are these relationships primarily transactional, or do they go deeper? What makes the difference?
- What agreements have you made, or what partnerships have you formed that have shaped your organisational journey?
- What constitutes progress on your journey? How do you discern the time, seasons, context, and terrain around you?
- How do you share your discoveries and learnings with others?

Americas

A participant from the USA said, "Living in California, the ongoing journey/story of immigrants is a powerful force in the culture […] this aspect of journey has more to do with interaction and ebb and flow between cultures that never really ends than a prescribed journey or voyage […] when looking at the phenomenon of migration of people – forced or otherwise. That journey-story continually unfolds."

One leader shared, "I am the grandchild and the great-grandchild of immigrants. My father's grandfather came to America from Denmark, along with other family, to live a new kind of life. My mother's father came to America from The Netherlands, with his siblings, for the same reason." He went on to share that his Dutch grandfather served in the US Army in WWI to earn his US citizenship and how both his grandfather and great-grandfather felt a desire for a radical change. There was a felt need to leave behind a difficult life with few prospects in hopes of new possibilities and potential opportunities. "From pilgrims seeking religious freedom to immigrants from other nations seeking the potential of creating their own, better life through hard work, all were willing to leave behind what [were] considered untenable living conditions, and to endure hardship and hard work for the hope of something better."

From Mexico, "In my family's culture, we place high importance on the past, so stories of journeys are mostly associated with what our ancestors experienced in their lives. Also important are significant transitions like: moving from the rural area to the city, marrying, having children, moving from being agnostic in matters of faith to becoming Christian, changes in economic and academic conditions."

- Leaders often need to make bold decisions. Have you been in such a situation? How did you navigate through it?
- Have you ever been in a situation where flight was the best option? How did you know it was the right choice, and how did you proceed to lead?

Going Deeper – Three Historical Journeys for Further Reflection

Central Europe, the Slovaks in Hungary

Deeply rooted even when displaced, Slovaks are among the few peoples who have lived in the same part of the world for thousands of years. Slovak history, in the region now known as Slovakia, can be traced back to 400 A.D. A Slovakian leader told the story of his ancestors, and many other Slovaks, moving to Hungary when their lives were endangered in their homeland because of the persecution of Protestants. Hungary welcomed them to work the difficult and empty land. The Slovaks invented methods of working the wet soil, and the land became fertile under their care. It was not until 300 years later, after World War II, that they returned to their homeland.

The history of the Slovak people is a part of the larger Slavic history. It may seem a chaotic, ever-changing picture for those not well-versed in this history. Paul Lendvai (2004) tracks the comings and goings and varying political views of the Slovak presence in Hungary. Sometimes appreciated, sometimes despised, the Slovaks continued their daily lives throughout the region under the rule of the Magyars and then the Hapsburg Empire. These rulers were followed by the Germans and then the Soviet Russians, until Slovakia finally became independent and also separated from the Czechs in the 1990s. This was such an intriguing story; I was compelled to learn more.

Thomas Capek's early twentieth century book on pan-Slavism sheds light on the long history of Slavic peoples, including the Slovaks. Capek states, "For centuries the Slovaks have inhabited Hungary, admittedly longer than the Magyars themselves, have fought and bled in defence of the fatherland jointly with others of their fellow-citizens. 'Liberty, equality, and fraternity of every citizen' is again our motto as it was a thousand years ago. This Slavic manifesto from the early 1800s defended the principle of equal rights" (Capek, 1906: 57). Everything changed, but nothing changed. Empires rose and fell over many centuries, with Slovakia, and eventually Hungary, in their power.

The non-Slavics feared pan-Slavism, fearing all the Slavic peoples would band together. While the Slavic people did seek unity where it was possible at various times in history, the various Slavic groups also had independent natures. They may have had common ground, but they valued their distinctives too much to just cast them aside. The Slovakian journey is a long and complex story. There are some intriguing similarities to the behaviour of the Israelites when they were captives in Babylon – accepting their current contexts, seeking the welfare of the society in which they lived, yet longing for and, generations later, returning home.

There are some intriguing similarities to the behaviour of the Israelites when they were captives in Babylon – accepting their current contexts, seeking the welfare of the society in which they lived, yet longing for and, generations later, returning home.

The Kom of Cameroon

African survey participant Paul Kimbi offered a summary of the history of his people, the Kom of Cameroon (Kimbi, 2018). One of the purposes of Kimbi's article (an excerpt from a longer paper) was to examine how events in Kom history and culture might have influenced their theological inclinations.

According to oral sources, the Kom people were wanderers until they sought refuge with another tribe of the Northwest Region of Cameroon, the Babessi. As the Kom became prosperous, the Babessi became jealous. They killed most of the working population of the Kom. Realising he had been tricked and was responsible for the deaths of many of his people, the Kom leader committed suicide. However, before he died, he gave several warnings to his remaining people, including that they should watch for a python trail that would appear after his death. They were expected to follow the trail wherever it led them. When it appeared, it led them through forest and savannah to their present location, a hilly savannah in the Northwest Region of Cameroon (Kimbi, 2018).

The influence of this journey story is still powerful among the Kom today. They have stayed closely linked to their history and traditions and still feel connected to their ancestors and to the python. They look to the past for wisdom. The Kom have persevered, and, for centuries, they have passed down this journey story of their origins. Kimbi notes that the influence of the Kom's journey stories can also help prepare their hearts and minds for the history of people's relationship with God. There are identifying points in the stories of the Jews leaving Egypt and going to the Promised Land and similarities found in other Bible stories as well. Journey is central to the story of the Kom people and is a connecting link to their understanding of Scripture as God's Good News unfolds before them.

Lewis and Clark, US Corps of Discovery

Citing the Lewis and Clark Expedition across North America, one survey participant commented that, in school, the expedition was described as a government mandate. However, the particulars of this journey "involved an astounding array of inventiveness displayed by those in the party and those they met along the way".

The Lewis and Clark story is, in a sense, also where this book's journey began. I was listening to the soundtrack from Ken Burns' documentary *Lewis & Clark: The Journey of the Corps of Discovery* while poring through strategic planning resources, preparing to help with strategy discussions in the newly formed Wycliffe Global Alliance. The more I read, the more I realised we needed to go where the music was taking me… on a journey. We were not fighting a war, competing with rivals, or building a high-rise empire. The Alliance was on a journey of discovery, together. Later, returning to the Lewis and Clark story, including the original expedition journals, I was more inspired than ever.

American history is story after story of journeys. In the US, we grew up on the stories of explorers, Native Americans, refugees, immigrants, and pioneers on the move. Most of the characters in these stories are ordinary people who faced the unknown and persevered through hardships, challenges, oppression, and/or tragedy. Some are the stories of our own families. People from around the world and from all walks of life made difficult ocean journeys. Many also walked or rode the long trails west. The story of the Lewis and Clark expedition is one of the best known of these stories.

Sent by President Thomas Jefferson in 1804 to find the fabled Northwest Passage, Meriwether Lewis and William Clark led a journey filled with danger, discovery, endless unknowns, and breathtaking scenery. Over a period of almost four years, they travelled from St. Louis to the headwaters of the Missouri River, over the Continental Divide to the Pacific Ocean, and back again. As American school children, we learned that the Lewis and Clark expedition wasn't just about the two captains. It was about the Corps of Discovery, a band of approximately fifty people, thirty-three of whom were considered the "permanent party" that made the entire journey. This party included young officers and enlisted men, hired frontiersmen, an African American enslaved man, a Shoshone mother, translators, French Canadian boatmen (Anderson, 1997), and a Newfoundland dog named Seaman (Couse, 1893: 332).

This diverse team accomplished what is considered the most important expedition in American history. Their wide-ranging skills equipped them, as well as any team could be prepared, to face the unknown. Numerous aspects of the Lewis and Clark journey make it worthy of study. Our brief look here focuses on their preparation and a few facets of leadership and team dynamics.

There was, of course, the preparation of goods for the journey. They gathered more than 2000 tons of equipment, everything from sextants to sewing needles, muzzle-loading rifles to mosquito curtains, kettles, forceps, flannel shirts, and a portable reference library (Anderson, 1997). The physical preparation was significant, but the mental preparation was equally impressive. In his book on the expedition, *Undaunted Courage*, Stephen Ambrose (1996) describes how Lewis became well-qualified to lead this journey. He was already an experienced and highly skilled soldier, frontiersman, leader, and explorer.

As Jefferson's secretary for several years, Lewis received a first-hand education in politics, history, navigation, philosophy, and literature. He read widely in Jefferson's expansive library. Ambrose states that Lewis was the perfect choice. "Indeed, Lewis's career might almost have been dedicated to preparing him for this adventure" (Ambrose, 1996:80). When ultimately choosing Lewis for the expedition, Jefferson and his Philadelphia scientist friends gave Lewis a crash course in astronomy, botany, mineralogy, medicine, cartography, and geography. Lewis' already keen eye was fine-tuned as he took on the documenting and cataloguing of flora and fauna along the journey and the responsibility for the Corps' forward progress. His mother Lucy had taught him herbal medicine and compassion. Lewis also became acquainted with and gained an understanding of the Native American groups he would encounter along the way (Couse, 1893: xxvii). The right resources, a good education, and a willingness to continue learning were critical factors in preparation.

> *The right resources, a good education, and a willingness to continue learning were critical factors in preparation.*

The leadership of the Corps was extraordinary in many ways. Jefferson entrusted Lewis with choosing the entire party and making any necessary decisions on the journey. Lewis chose William Clark, not as his second-in-command, but as co-commander. Ambrose states, "Divided command almost never works and is the bane of military men, to whom the sanctity of the chain of command is basic and the idea of two disagreeing commanders in a critical situation is anathema. But Lewis did it anyway" (1996: 97-99). Lewis and Clark had a long history of service together and their robust, complementary relationship would, in the end, play a significant part in sustaining the Corps. They had complete trust in each other and knew each other's strengths and weaknesses.

Lewis and Clark had many men to choose from for the expedition (Clarke, 1970: 1617). Clark, deemed an excellent judge of character, gathered some of the "best young woodsmen and Hunters in this part of the Countrey [*sic*]" (Ambrose, 1996: 105). (Note: spelling was not standardised in Clark's era.) The men had great confidence in their leaders. Ambrose talks about the relative absence of rumours among the men as they travelled, encountering and enduring the stress of one unknown after another. The men completely trusted Lewis and Clark (Ambrose, 1996: 245).

Ambrose and other historians provide ample evidence as to why Lewis and Clark's men were so willing to follow. They cite Lewis's sensitivity to morale, Clark's rapport with the enlisted men, their care and concern for the travellers' physical and emotional well-being, and their willingness to work alongside them, even cooking for them (Ambrose, 1996: 411). "Once, at the end of the Great Portage around the Falls of the Missouri, Lewis became the cook of the Corps' White Bear Islands Camp. After cutting his own wood and hauling water for the fire, he prepared a feast for the men of roasted buffalo meat, and even made each man a large suet dumpling by way of a treat" (Anderson, 1997). In a culture and era of rank and hierarchy, such behaviours were uncommon in the military or any group. Serving the common good and common goal through serving his men, Lewis kept the expedition's goals in mind and showed concern for the expedition's people.

Even though the captains were in positions of authority, they paid attention to the opinions of their enlisted men, many of whom had extensive knowledge and intuition about the wilderness. In November 1805, having reached the West Coast, they needed to decide where to spend the winter. "The captains decide to put the matter to a vote. Significantly, in addition to the others, Clark's enslaved assistant, York, is allowed to vote – nearly 60 years before enslaved people in the US would be emancipated and enfranchised. Sacagawea, the Native American woman, votes too – more than a century before either women or Native Americans are granted full rights of citizenship" (Anderson, 1997).

They built winter quarters near what is modern day Astoria, Oregon, and in spring, began the long return journey. This round-trip journey, the relationships built along the way, and all the information gathered, made many more journeys possible, both round-trip and one-way. We continue to follow their trails, on foot and in our cars. We see the breathtaking mountains and the Pacific and imagine what it must have been like to see them unexpectedly and for the first time. Our journey is different, but we learn from those who went before us.

> Whilst I viewed those mountains, I felt a secret pleasure in finding myself so near the head of the – heretofore conceived – boundless Missouri. But when I reflected on the difficulties which this snowy barrier would most probably throw in my way to the Pacific Ocean, and the sufferings and hardships of myself and the party in them, it in some measure counterbalanced the joy I had felt in the first moments in which I gazed on them. But, as I have always held it little short of criminality to anticipate evils, I will allow it to be a good, comfortable road until I am compelled to believe otherwise. Meriwether Lewis (Couse, 1893: 328).

- What leadership lessons can be learned from the journeys of the Slovaks? The Kom people? Lewis and Clark?
- What values, training, and qualifications shape your leadership?
- What similarities do you see between the Israelites' exile in Babylon and the example of the Slovaks in Hungary? How does clarity of identity impact their attitudes and behaviour?
- The Kom value their history and traditions. How does your journey story impact your ideas and decisions?
- How did Lewis and Clark's decisions about preparation, people, and resources shape their journey?
- Lewis and Clark set an example of co-leadership. Such leadership is still not the norm, but is becoming more accepted. Where have you seen it work or not work? Do you think it would work in your organisation? Why or why not? What would be some of the potential pros and cons?

5. Journey and Scripture

Walk in a manner worthy of the Lord, fully pleasing to him: bearing fruit in every good work and increasing in the knowledge of God; being strengthened with all power, according to his glorious might, for all endurance and patience with joy.

Colossians 1:10-11

Overview

> *To travel well, we need to continue learning about the character of the God who leads us.*

As we see how journey is portrayed in God's Word, we will also gain wisdom for applying the journey concept to our participation in God's mission. To travel well, we need to continue learning about the character of the God who leads us. We can also benefit from exploring the many lessons in the stories of those called to follow him.

What We Heard... and Didn't Hear

Question 11 of the Journey Survey asked: "What stories or passages in the Bible that deal with the concept of journey are significant to you, and why?" There are many journey stories in Scripture, but it is intriguing to see which ones the survey participants cited. This global array of leaders often mentioned the same stories but expressed a wide range of lessons learned and examples to follow.

As you read what is presented here, take time for additional reflection. Our tendencies and training often lead us to focus more on the biblical narrative's human characters than on God's character. We may more easily relate to the wonderings and frailties of these men and women, but our relationship is with the same God they either knew or rejected. Note what you can learn about God: who he is and how he acts in our world and in the lives of his people. Your missional intent will grow clearer. Your feet will be better prepared for the path ahead. And you will grow in both the leadership and followership to which you have been called.

Old Testament

EARLY STORIES

Although it might be considered the first journey, no one mentioned Adam and Eve's banishment from the garden. Several leaders mentioned Noah's voyage, questioning whether or not it was a true journey as there was no destination in mind. One stated that Noah's actual journey was a faith journey through forty years of patient obedience and building a vessel beyond the comprehension or belief of his neighbours. For our purposes, we will identify Noah's voyage as fitting the flight category of journey. Forty days at sea in the first and greatest flood ever, with a boatload of creatures and extended family, certainly seems to qualify as a physical journey of some sort, as well as the faith journey mentioned above.

One leader mentioned a journey often overlooked because of greater focus on the event, the building of the Tower of Babel. Although it might not be the first journey-related Scripture passage to come to mind, the story is bookended with journeys. Genesis 11:2 says the people journeyed from the east and settled on a plain in the land of Shinar. There, they began building a city and a tower, desiring to make a name for themselves, so they would not be scattered across the earth. God, however, had other plans for them. He "confused" their language so that they spoke different languages. Without the ability to understand one another, the people gave up on the city, tower, and (for a time) their aspirations for greatness, and "the Lord scattered them abroad over the face of the earth" (Gen. 11:9).

Several survey participants mentioned Abraham's literal and metaphorical journeys. Some mentioned his faith in undertaking the journey, setting off into a new future for his people, meeting God, and interacting with his newfound neighbours.

Joseph's journeys, as described in Genesis, were noted. "[H]is relationship with God shaped his character, behaviour, and decisions. His cheerful spirit allowed him to live in adverse circumstances throughout his life." "Big dreams in the beginning. Typical of young people. [They] want people to say [that they] are a star. It did happen but through a difficult humbling journey."

Several participants reflected on Job. One leader said Job's journey was not one of distances but of suffering, pain, and growth. Another said, "I really appreciate the changes in Job and the conclusion he finally comes to. I can identify, to my chagrin, with his friends and all their good advice and wholeheartedly admire and wish to surrender as completely to God as [Job] did." Another mentions Job's unwavering faith in God, unwilling to give up his faith despite his circumstances. There was also mention of David's journey from shepherd to king and Jonah's journeys of rebellion and repentance.

Few leaders mentioned women of the Bible. There was no mention of Sarah journeying with Abraham or Miriam traveling with and helping lead the

Israelites. Nor was there mention of Rebekah's journey to join Isaac. One leader cited Ruth, "her willingness to follow God in a strange language and culture, a remarkable woman". Deborah was also noted: "[She had a] clear vision of her own role as a leader in her society and culture, and a total dependence on God for all decisions in her life and for her people."

- Have you ever had to change plans, venture out, start something new? Were you surprised by how your course was changed, how far you went, or how differently things turned out than expected? How did you see God at work in ways you might not have seen otherwise?
- How does your relationship with God shape you, your behaviours, attitudes, and decisions?

Exodus stories

The most frequently mentioned journey stories were those of the Israelites, primarily the accounts of God leading Moses and the Israelites out of Egypt, through the wilderness, and into the Promised Land. Survey participants spoke of lessons learned through these stories.

It was an "amazing journey that reveals God's heart for his people and the great lengths he is willing to go to shape them […] for his purpose […]. [This] gives me courage to stay the course despite having to wrestle issues both personal and in my work."

"Walking through the wilderness can be a good thing, a time to learn how God is working, without the distraction of thinking I'm in control. From Deuteronomy 8:4 [there is] this small detail of the Israelites' time of wilderness wandering: 'your garments did not wear out on you, nor your foot swell these 40 years.'" God's miraculous provision extended far beyond manna and quail. Durable clothes and tough feet may not seem like miracles, until you need them.

- How has God provided in practical ways along your journey as an individual or an organisation?
- What have you had to learn "the hard way"? What have you learned about God?

Survey participants reflected on Moses' character and actions. One mentioned the importance of Moses' time as a shepherd in the desert. Another leader noted that before the exodus, there was Moses' journey back to Egypt after many years away and that Moses answered God's call and command even though he felt inadequate and scared. "Moses was a man of prayer leading a difficult and enormous group of people." "Moses' faith in God allowed him to see Christ and [he] considered that suffering for the Messiah was better than the treasures of Egypt." "Without his obedience the people were stuck. His journey with them started toward the Promised Land." One leader stated that Moses began not knowing where he was going. It was not a planned journey but was taken in obedience to God. In doing this, Moses was able to impact a whole nation, although that was not his plan. Making himself available to God, he was changed in the process and changed the course of the Israelites' history.

- As you reflect, look at God's role in this journey. Moses may not have started with a plan, but God certainly did! What is God's role in your journey?

Although most survey participants chose to mention Moses and the exodus as their example of a journey in Scripture, there was still great variety in their impressions and learnings. Many focused on the Israelites' experience. One leader considered the failings of the Israelites, saying their journey was "an unnecessarily long journey that should have been completed in less time if the people had trusted God." Another shared a different perspective, citing that the Israelites' dramatic and rushed escape demonstrated reliance on God and his deliverance.

Having witnessed the Pacific Islanders' strong connection with the land in earlier chapters of this book, it is no surprise that survey participants from the Pacific see land issues in the exodus and Babylonian captivity narratives. A Pacific Island leader shared, "[They] became a threat to the land owners. But the Lord who owns the world and all that is in it (Psalm 24) gave it to them. We must honour and obey the Lord. If we do not, he will evict us from the land; just like the Israelites who turned to worship other gods. God gave them up into captivity."

Also, from the Pacific, "Israelites leave Egypt for the land of promise. This tells me God has given a physical map for his own people to the destination place. But not only that. He also wants them to understand the spiritual destination, which is their hearts full of the knowledge of God and them worshipping God alone. The spiritual journey is most important for the Israelites because it determined whether they would reach their physical destination." This powerful statement connects the spiritual journey with the outcome of the physical journey.

Several leaders mentioned that we often act toward God in the same ways as the Israelites. One reflected, "The most significant [story] for me is that of the Israelites from Egypt to Canaan. It signifies, in many ways, my own journey in my Christian life. There are many lessons to draw from it:

- the freedom it gave them;
- the challenges in the wilderness;
- the unexpected events they had to deal with;
- the miraculous provisions time and time again;
- and most of all God's promise that he would be with them, even when they so easily forgot."

Leaders also noted the story's connections to community. One related the exodus story, from slavery to freedom, to the history of the Philippines through colonial times and the martial law regime. Another said, "Israel's journey to the promised land illustrates the journey of a community, and now of the Church. It also shows God's relationship and care for them by providing the cloud and fire to guide them." The resources needed could not be foretold but became available as needed. Dependency on God was the only guarantee of a secure outcome of the journey.

Dependency on God was the only guarantee of a secure outcome of the journey.

Several participants mentioned the journey of the spies to Canaan. "Joshua and Caleb went on a God-to-Moses directed mission, but maintained a vision when others did not for the place they saw that involved a faith in the unseen and unshakeable trust in the Lord." This was the beginning of the examples set by the next generation of leaders.

- Where have you seen next-generation leadership maintaining the vision while also moving forward in new ways? How have you or could you encourage them? What have you learned from them?

New Testament

JESUS' LIFE

Joseph and Mary's journey to Bethlehem was the first of the New Testament journeys cited by survey participants. One leader noted that their journey was instrumental in fulfilling the biblical prophecy concerning where Jesus would be born. Another mentioned the journey of the Magi and said, "[T]hey remind [me] of our ancestors because they understood how to read and understand the seasons, stars, and [God's] creation". One leader shared learnings from Luke 15:11-32, the story of the prodigal son. "When life gets tough, returning home is the wise thing to do. You have a home, family, and a land to return to where you will be welcome even if the welcome is unpleasant."

Numerous people mentioned Jesus' journeys:

- Incarnation – "God's journey to dwell in my neighbourhood."
- "Jesus travelled with the disciples and sent the disciples in pairs."
- Jesus' return to Jerusalem and his last week of ministry culminating in all he had come to earth to do, his triumphal arrival, last supper, sentencing by Pilate, crucifixion, and resurrection.
- His journey to the cross in his final days – his focus, commitment, compassion, and persistence to reach the cross and fulfil his purpose.
- "He never forgot the reason for his journey – people."
- The road to Emmaus is another example of Jesus journeying and spending time with people. His fellow travellers were always learning along the way.

THE APOSTLES

Peter's spiritual journey inspired several survey participants.

Peter's life was significant as a "lifelong journey of missional conversion [...]. He started as a clumsy 'act before think' disciple in the gospels". One participant goes on to reflect on how Christ's resurrection had a major impact on Peter and notes the 3000 people that repented on hearing Peter's Pentecost sermon. "Yet he had a long journey ahead."

Noting how the epistles Peter wrote in his later years show evidence of his spiritual maturity, "Peter's story is significant in that nobody in this world has completed his/her share of spiritual maturation (the full measure of Christ) and thus everyone should humbly keep marching on with his/her own journey."

The Apostle Paul and his journeys were the most referenced Bible stories in the survey responses. Participants readily shared their insights.

Paul's example showed his heart and head "full of passion and practical love and persistent focus on the purpose of his journey, yet a man who makes himself sensitive to the Holy Spirit and the Word and develops intimate friendships with his team mates". One participant said this example taught him about "the intrinsic importance of relationships with God and companions and the importance of the relationships to achieving purpose and reaching the destination". Another said, "Paul taught about our nature as pilgrims, journeying through the earth, which is not our place of citizenship."

Some survey participants focused on Paul's mission.

One wrote of "Paul and the missionary bands" and how the gospel was deliberately taken from the Jewish context to the Gentiles throughout Asia Minor. The church was planted and grew as people were discipled and leaders mentored. Another stated, "Paul's missionary journeys show how central journeying is to communicating the gospel and announcing the coming of the kingdom of God."

Several participants found Paul's race inspirational.

One leader referenced 2 Timothy 4:7-8, noting, "God used Paul and led him on an amazing journey of missionary work and writing scripture. Hope for a sinner and God able to use one's background [and] gifts for his purposes. Paul had a clear desire to finish the race; he had found the purpose for his life and presses on – forgetting what lies behind and pressing on to what lies ahead."

"[W]e are called to leave our routine, possibly our home and home country, to go and make disciples; following God's call means going on journeys – with all the planning, discomfort, and comfort it brings."

"Paul's passionate desire to preach the gospel to the Jews and Gentiles to the extent of being persecuted himself sets the example for being a follower of Christ [...]. I [too] have a journey with God since I surrendered my life to him."

Some leaders took a big picture approach.

"Christianity at its core is a traveling religion where a lot of the significant figures are travelling people."

"Moses led his people to a specific destination, Jesus travelled with the purpose of meeting people and giving the Great Commandment that sparked the idea of the travelling movement, and Paul, who travelled to share the gospel."

"There is a journey from suffering on earth to no suffering in heaven."

One leader cited James 1:2-4 and Romans 5:3-5 as personally significant passages. "I have gone through lots of trials and tribulations and such have built my character in terms of perseverance, patience and hope. James is a powerful and practical manual on applying our faith in Christ to the struggles and relationships we encounter every day."

A leader noted Hebrews 11:13 as significant because "our forefathers in faith recognised they were foreigners on earth. That hope made them live expecting things that were promised and at the same time realistic about who they were." Another stated that, as a traveller, you don't forget where you come from. The leader also mentioned 1 Peter 2:11 and the concept of strangers on earth, reminding us that we are also strangers when we travel to another place. "That passage is significant to me because it invites us to live Christ-like lives."

One participant shared, "It is interesting to note how much of Scripture involves incidents that happened when people were travelling. I don't think this is coincidental. God can meet us more easily when we have left our usual surroundings behind but have not yet arrived at a new place, we have more time and perhaps more need of assistance in this in-between phase."

Another leader responded, "The whole Bible is a journey of God's plan and purpose for the fallen world, starting with calling the people through Abraham to Himself to lead and demonstrate His love to a fallen world."

Reading and applying what the survey participants shared could supply enough material for numerous books and reflections. They have taken these stories to heart, learned from them, and are encouraged by them. They see journey as not just theme but reality. Each Bible story and character provide wisdom and lessons applicable to life today.

- How can you or you and your team benefit from the survey participants' learnings and make time to explore these stories anew?

Sojourners and Strangers

Christians have often been known as, or called themselves, sojourners, pilgrims, "strangers in a strange land". What does that mean? Sojourner is sometimes understood to mean a traveller, someone passing through, perhaps staying a while, but planning to move on. Sojourners are sometimes portrayed in contrast to settlers, with settlers being those who come and plan to stay. With immigration issues in the news worldwide, the discussion of biblical treatment of immigrants, sojourners, and various other categories of "strangers in our midst" is lively (often with the recognition that those who are the resident citizens are little different from the newcomers, just separated by a few generations).

In the Old Testament, sojourners are recognised resident aliens, noncitizens of the country in which they live. Some English translations use "foreigners" or "strangers". Whatever word is used, there's always the sense of otherness. In Genesis 23:4, "Abraham says, 'I am a sojourner and foreigner among you; give me property among you for a burying place, that I may bury my dead out of my sight.'" God had already told him his offspring would also be sojourners (Gen. 15:13). There are many Old Testament references to sojourners. The Israelites spent generations as sojourners themselves and were also instructed in how to treat the sojourners who came their way.

According to Old Testament laws, sojourners were to be provided for, well-treated, and subject to most of the same laws as the Israelites. "For the assembly, there shall be one statute for you and for the stranger who sojourns with you, a statute forever throughout your generations. You and the sojourner shall be alike before the Lord" (Num. 15:15). This speaks to more than abiding by laws, however, as it demonstrates God's view of citizen and sojourner as equal. Deuteronomy 10:19 instructs, "Love the sojourner, therefore, for you were sojourners in the land of Egypt." And, "When you gather the grapes of your vineyard, you shall not strip it afterward. It shall be for the sojourner, the fatherless, and the widow" (Dt. 24:21). Often listed along with the fatherless and the widow, sojourners were a reminder to the Israelites of their own history and vulnerability; with this in mind, the Israelites were to treat sojourners as God had treated them.

Although sojourners sometimes spend most of their lives in an "adopted" country or a specific community, they might always have a sense of being "other". There may be a longing for home or recognition of being somehow set apart. The Israelites seemed to understand they were still sojourners and guests even when they had a home. "For we are strangers before you and sojourners, as all our fathers were. Our days on the earth are like a shadow, and there is no abiding" (1 Chr. 29:15). "Hear my prayer, O Lord, and give ear to my cry; hold not your peace at my tears! For I am a sojourner with you, a guest, like all my fathers" (Ps. 39:12).

The theme continues in the New Testament.

"Beloved, I urge you as sojourners and exiles to abstain from the passions of the flesh, which wage war against your soul" (1 Pt. 2:11). From the very beginning of the book, 1 Peter has a continuing theme of strangers/exiles/pilgrims.

Hebrews gives the big picture, the long historical list of sojourners who died in faith, looking toward the "not yet". "These all died in faith, not having received the things promised, but having seen them and greeted them from afar, and having acknowledged that they were strangers and exiles on the earth [...]. But as it is, they desire a better country, that is, a heavenly one. Therefore God is not ashamed to be called their God, for he has prepared for them a city" (Heb.

11:13, 16). "Here we have no lasting city, but we seek the city that is to come" (Heb. 13:14).

In a sense, Ephesians 2:18-19 offers an even bigger picture when, in speaking to the Gentiles, Paul says, "For through him we both have access in one Spirit to the Father. So then you are no longer strangers and aliens, but you are fellow citizens with the saints and members of the household of God."

To call yourself a sojourner is an acknowledgment of belonging to somewhere else, and that you are not in your true home. You are on a journey. It doesn't mean that you are constantly on the move, a ceaseless traveller, or uncaring of the context around you. This distinction is clearly depicted in God's instructions to the Israelites when taken captive to Babylon. "Thus says the Lord God of hosts, the God of Israel, to all the exiles whom I have sent into exile from Jerusalem to Babylon: Build houses and live in them; plant gardens and eat their produce. Take wives and have sons and daughters" (Jr. 29:4-6). The passage continues as God tells the people to "seek the welfare of the city where I have sent you" (v.7), and to pray for it because the Israelites' welfare depended on its welfare (Jr. 29:7). Theologians Hauerwas and Wilimon spoke of the church as being in this same sort of state, calling it an "adventure" to be the church, "people who reside here and now, but who live here as aliens, who know that, while we live here, our commonwealth is in heaven" (2014: 29).

In chapter 3, we identified three types of journeys:

- Round-trip – coming home – what will you bring back?
- One-way – a new destination – where will you go?
- Flight – leaving is the goal – how will you survive?

As a forced journey, the story of the Babylonian Captivity would fall in the flight journey category. Although they would someday return home, the Israelites' focus for the next five hundred years was, "How will we survive?" God answered that question quite clearly through Jeremiah. He depicts the sojourners making the most of life in a country or location not their own, living as if it were home, and working for the well-being of all. This is an important aspect of the journey. The road does not always lead where you thought you were going. And not every part of the journey may find you literally on the road or in motion. But, at every point, God is directing and leading.

How does this connect with the journey concept, missional intent, and strategy? Numerous Scripture passages and the example of Christ in Scripture point us toward caring about our context even as we are "passing through". God instructed the exiles to be supportive of their country of exile. Jesus certainly took time to give attention to the people around him, even though he was focused on a larger goal and would not be on earth for long. All the instructions and examples point toward being aware, attentive, and good stewards of all we are given. They also point to being present, to participating in community. Even when looking toward the future, there are homes to create, gardens to plant, children to care for, and prayers to say in the course of everyday life.

These aspects of being a sojourner, or being on a journey, speak to the importance of reflective practice. Understanding your purpose and place, developing a humble attitude, and exercising stewardship may not be the first responsibilities that come to mind when you think of a journey. However, as a sojourner, a follower of Christ in the now and future kingdom, they are critical considerations. Hauerwas and Wilimon state, "Christianity is more than a matter of a new understanding. Christianity is an invitation to be a part of an alien people who make a difference because they see something that cannot otherwise be seen without Christ" (24: 2014). This raises the question: have we been missing something by being so absorbed into the secular business mindset?

Pilgrims and Pioneers

Words like sojourner, stranger, exile, foreigner, and alien are used in most English translations of the Bible, but many of their characteristics could also be applied to pilgrims and pioneers. The word *pilgrim* does appear in some translations. As we have seen from Scripture and the stories told by survey participants, there are many whose journeys (literal or figurative) take them to new places, on quests, back home again, or to a new home far from where they began. These are the round-trip or one-way journeys, the journeys of pilgrims and pioneers.

God sent Abram on a one-way journey. "Go from your country and your kindred and your father's house to the land that I will show you" (Gen. 12:1). Psalm 84:5 (NIV) says, "Blessed are those whose strength is in you, whose hearts are set on pilgrimage." The ESV says, "Blessed are those whose strength is in you, in whose heart are the highways to Zion." The original Hebrew was closer to "in whose heart are the steeps (or highways)" (Strong, 2009: 4546). Although the wording is different, each conveys a sense of longing. This is the signature of the pilgrim.

Bosch stated, "The church is viewed as the *people of God* and by implication then, as a *pilgrim* church" (1991: 373). Called out of the world and sent back to the world, "it is permanently underway" (1991: 374). He also said that God's pilgrim people need only two things for the road: "support for the road" and "a destination at the end of it" (1991: 374). "We live within the creative tension of the already and the not yet" (Bosch, 1979: 85). Unlike the wanderers and seekers who often walk the historical pilgrimage trails today with an unidentified longing and in hopes of finding purpose, God's pilgrim people travel with a purpose and with a longing that is focused on a growing relationship and a promised destination.

And what of the pioneers? The Christ followers most often referred to as pioneers are the missionaries who have gone to places and peoples considered dangerous – or at least unknown – to the sending community. Unfortunately, many people through the years have blurred the line between mythically-proportioned explorers and simply obedient missionaries. However, neither the explorers nor the missionaries were usually the intrepid loners so often portrayed. Not meaning to disrespect their efforts in any way, it should still be noted that behind, alongside, and often in front of these notables, were (usually) less-noted colleagues, teammates who helped make it possible. Nor were most pioneers individualists who braved new territory alone. More often, they were families and newfound or longtime friends who travelled together, helped each other, and circled their wagons for the security and safety of the community each night. Professor George Greenia, founder of the William & Mary Institute for Pilgrimage Studies, noted the same of the pilgrim, stating that pilgrimage "has always been a powerful gesture of group spirituality" (2018: 8), and "invites, even requires a surrender of individualism" (2018: 12). Most Christ followers do not go out alone, but seek the companionship and support of others who are like-minded. This is an important factor as we speak of journey. It is not a solitary effort. Although not all make the physical journey, the journey is made in community, with colleagues, in collaboration. We are in this together.

On the Way, דרך Derekh and ὁδός Hodos

John Calvin wrote, "We are always on the road." A displaced refugee himself, it is said he never felt truly at home, even in Geneva, although he became an official citizen there near the end of his life (George, 2011: 252). "Calvin preached and wrote for sojourners, refugees, and emigrants, for pilgrims who like Abraham and Sarah of old were looking for a city whose builder and maker was God" (George, 2011: 253). So, although his reference to being "on the road" was autobiographical, it was first and foremost a reflection of what he knew from Scripture.

The two words, *derekh*, Hebrew, and *hodos*, Greek, have a common meaning related to journey. *Derekh* (Strong, 2009: 1870) is the transliteration of the Hebrew word for "way, road, path, journey". Danker defines *hodos* as "an established 'way' or 'course', such as a road or channel of a river. A way for travelling or moving from one place to another (way, road, highway). The action of travelling, way, trip, journey. It is a course of behaviour, way, way of life, way of acting, conduct. Of the whole way of life, a moral or spiritual viewpoint" (2000: 691-92).

Derekh and *hodos* are used in a variety of ways in Scripture. Like the English word *journey*, they can serve as nouns or verbs and be literal or metaphorical.

Matthew 2:12 tells of God warning the Magi about Herod, after which "they departed to their own country by another *way*" (italics added). In this example, the way is a literal road or route for travelling.

Just a few verses but some years later in Matthew 3:3, Matthew tells of John the Baptist fulfilling the prophecy of Isaiah, as a voice calling in the wilderness, "Prepare the *way* of the Lord, make his paths straight" (italics added). John the Baptist taught repentance, encouraged spiritual thinking and growth, and reminded the people of what Scripture said. In a sense, the *way* represents the preparation of the people's hearts and minds for the coming Messiah. Making straight paths would be clearing out "debris", helping people focus on God and his promises.

John 14:6, "I am the *way*, the truth and the life" (italics added). In this passage, Jesus is announcing he is the Way, the one for whom Israel has been waiting. Those who follow will find salvation, eternal life. He is the Way and the teacher of the way.

Paul frequently spoke of the *way*. In 1 Thessalonians 3:11, Paul expresses his desire to see the Thessalonians again. The *way* is both the route and the means. Finding a way can mean making something possible. In 1 Corinthians 12:31, he speaks of "a still more excellent *way*" (italics added). Here, Paul is preparing to tell the Corinthians that the way of love is superior to other gifts. The way, in this case, is a preferred approach to life. Hebrews 10:19-20, "new and living *way*" (italics added) follows that same direction, but the way here can refer to a way of life and to Christ himself.

Paul, in Acts 24:14, says, "according to the Way". Here and in several other passages, the Way refers to the whole way of life, believing in Christ and worshipping God. "The Way" was how some people of that time referred to the new "religion", sect, or faith of those who followed Christ.

In these examples, we again see journey as reality and metaphor, a physical road and an approach to living. We see the *way* as referring to behaviours and beliefs, and as referring to Christ himself. The use of the term *hodos* as a journey, a path, or a way of life, indicates a sense of progression, a connectedness, something pursued with consistency and commitment. There is nothing random to it. Learning about sojourners and pilgrims helps us focus on purpose and place. *Hodos* has much to teach us about path and posture/position.

For the believer and for an organisation, church, or movement of believers, both the journey and the destination matter.

For the believer and for an organisation, church, or movement of believers, both the journey and the destination matter. We are on our way to God and he is with us. As Tennent states, "Salvation involves becoming full participants in the New Creation, which is already breaking through the present order" (2010: 222). It is part of kingdom come and coming. That's why we don't want to miss any of it.

Walking Together

When the Wycliffe Global Alliance was forming and exploring new ways of being and working, the journey metaphor quickly proved useful and relatable. Not surprisingly, transportation metaphors entered the discussion. The leadership looked at Alex Araujo and Werner Mischke's powerboat and sailboat metaphors from their models on power-based control. The sailboat represented shared control, working together as a team, and reliance on the Holy Spirit, the "wind" or force that guides and enables God's mission. The powerboat represented reliance on speed and efficiency and was often seen as the Western way of doing things (Franklin, 2017: 107). Proponents of the powerboat model operate in a self-reliant, high-control manner dependent upon management methods and technology. This mindset influences most Christian ministries in some form or another, "from strategic planning and management – to evangelism and church planting – to donor relations and fund-raising" (Araujo & Mischke, 2009: 2). Another article by Araujo, Lederleitner, and Mischke pointed out that external conditions are the same, regardless of the boat. "The seas are what they are and the weather will be what it will be" (2008: 2). It's the vessel that makes the difference. There is a difference in design, training, and the journey. Perhaps, most importantly, there is a difference in mindset.

Leaders from the Global South and East, in particular, were drawn to the sailboat metaphor. Many had experienced (often unpleasant) encounters with the powerboat model. Powerboat/sailboat metaphors are helpful in many contexts where power is an issue. And power is an issue most of the time in most of the world. Colleagues around the world resonated with these metaphors, and feeling, in a sense, freed by this open discussion of power issues, they came up with other metaphors to help convey their thoughts and emotions and to also portray the history of what they had experienced.

At a global meeting of Alliance leaders, in response to the powerboat/sailboat concept, a Latin American colleague presented the idea that, previously, Northern/Western organisations had been in fast cars. "Now we are all on the bus together!" Many could identify with the camaraderie of bus rides and also with long and sometimes treacherous bus rides where the passengers' mental, physical, and emotional well-being are closely tied to the driver's skills. The bus offers an image of community, trust, and dependence on God. These discussions, greatly helped by metaphors, led to many other fruitful conversations and contributed much to the journey of the Alliance.

In considering the power of these metaphors, we can reflect on which modes of transportation might be most helpful in portraying leadership and the journey concept. Walking keeps coming to mind. There is a lot in Scripture about walking. Walking still has a certain appeal; it allows for companionship, conversation, reflection, appreciation of creation, varied pacing, and refreshment.

An often-recited essay entitled "One Solitary Life", usually attributed to James Allan Francis (1864–1928), describes Jesus' life as one of obscurity, and says, "He never put his foot inside a big city. He never travelled two hundred miles from the place where He was born" (Francis, 2016). This idea, popularised by others as well, of Jesus as a country boy, sticking close to home, is a bit misleading. One, he was far from home just in the fact that he came to Earth. Two, Jerusalem was a large city for its day. And three, although Jesus may not have travelled vast distances, it is estimated that he walked a minimum of 15,000 miles in his lifetime on Earth (Hargis, 1998). So, while the essay points out that Jesus did not do many things the world associates with greatness, Jesus was definitely on a journey, and his physical journey was primarily on foot. There were occasional boat rides and at least one donkey, but Jesus spent most of his days walking with his disciples and, often, great crowds. Tracking Christ through all four gospels is a worthy study. For now, we will take a brief sampling of the book of Matthew and see what happens as he walks.

Matthew 3 – Jesus' first action as an adult, he "came from Galilee to be baptised".

Matthew 4 – Led by the Spirit into the wilderness, he went to Galilee when he heard John was imprisoned, moved to Capernaum by the sea.

Matthew 4:18-22 – As he was walking, he called the disciples.

Matthew 4:23 – He went throughout all of Galilee, teaching, preaching, healing, and the crowds followed him.

Matthew 9:9, 27, 35 – "[A]s Jesus went on from there"; the calling of Matthew; eating with sinners; telling stories; answering questions; restoring; healing; teaching; preaching through the villages.

Matthew 14:22-25 – Jesus sent disciples back in the boat, dispersed the crowd, went up to the mountain to pray alone, and walked on the water.

Matthew 21:1 – When they approached Jerusalem…

In our world of speed, innovation, and urgency, it is essential to remember the value of walking. Theologian and missionary Kosuke Koyama wrote a book of reflections entitled *Three Mile an Hour God*. "God walks 'slowly' because he is love. If he is not love, he would have gone much faster. Love has its speed. It is an inner speed. It is a spiritual speed […]. It goes on in the depth of our life, whether we notice or not, whether we are currently hit by a storm or not, at three miles an hour. It is the speed we walk and therefore it is the speed the love of God walks" (1979: 7). Immanuel, God with us.

This is what makes our journey possible.

6. Leadership and the Journey of Missional Intent

> The fatal metaphor of progress, which means leaving things behind us, has utterly obscured the real idea of growth, which means leaving things inside us.
>
> *G.K. Chesterton, Orthodoxy*

Introduction

In this final chapter, we will explore several key issues and challenges common to most leaders. We will look further at the journey alongside missional intent, and the role of the journey leader in light of God's mission. We will also explore how the journey concept, with a missional basis, can impact a leader's thinking and responses.

We have seen how people worldwide comprehend journey as both metaphor and reality, inseparable from life experience. The near-universal yet highly personal understanding of journey enriches the concept with a wealth of perspectives that go deep and broad. Recognising the reality of the journey enriches our theological perspective and informs our day-to-day practices.

God as Leader

We've established a context for the journey concept. The concept can be used in many ways and under many conditions. However, we have chosen to evaluate it in a Christian context wherein we understand our life/ministry as participation with God in his mission. We understand our journey as under God's direction. We understand missional intent as our best efforts, under God's leading, to discern, as leaders and in community, how God desires us to participate.

Discernment comes through listening and watching to see what God is doing, how he is preparing and equipping us. Discernment comes through prayer, reflection, and community response. It requires that we be attuned to God, the world around us, and those we serve and serve with. We recognise our call, as followers, to participation in kingdom ministry: God's mission. We understand participation as being and doing, with an emphasis on reflective practice. In this chapter, we will look more closely at the how and why of journey leadership, particularly in contrast to the methods and measurements often promoted by the corporate influences we regularly encounter.

The starting point of this discussion is the recognition of God as leader. God is in charge. It is his mission. He leads it. As a colleague once said, "This changes everything!" Our organisations and movements, our churches, are not really ours. Anything and anyone that serves God's kingdom belongs to God. Knowing God is in charge relieves us of the burden of thinking we must be in control, have answers to everything, and be able to see the future. Leaders can become discouraged and even desperate when they have to acknowledge that no human can establish or maintain complete control. However, knowing we have a Leader capable of all that and so much more means that there is hope. God's future for us is already secured and he will be glorified. Furthermore, this means that leaders under his authority have the benefit of his wisdom and direction but must also learn to follow.

> *Knowing God is in charge relieves us of the burden of thinking we must be in control.*

Leaders Following the Leader

Christopher Wright stated, "The ethical challenge to God's people is, first, to recognise the mission of God that provides the heartbeat of their very existence and, then, to respond in ways that express and facilitate it rather than deny and hinder it" (2006: 357).

A leader has the privilege of helping create an environment wherein God's people can respond to his leading. In addition to all we can learn from Scripture, there are many excellent books and articles on Christian leadership. Some of the more recent resources particularly relate to trinitarian missional theology, the growth of the global church, and its diversity.

Franklin (2017: 150) addresses the formation of a global missional mindset, identifying the characteristics of missional leadership as:

- discerning with the Holy Spirit and God's community what God is doing in the world;
- dwelling in God's Word and living within the narrative of Scripture;
- imagining what God wants to do in the world;
- an inner transformation of the leader and those they lead.

Niemandt looks at leadership for the missional church, stating, "Jesus does not call leaders, but calls followers to follow him [...]. This church, as a band of faithful followers, is called by the Spirit to be on a journey with God" (2019a: loc 1626). He defines missional leadership as "the transformation of people and institutions to participate, through meaningful relations and in the power of the Spirit, in God's mission" (2019a: loc 1137). Niemandt also relates missional leadership to the journey, characterising it as relational and spiritual, and commenting that missional spirituality is a spirituality for the road (reflecting on

Bosch's book of the same title). It is robust enough to be carried into everyday life (Niemandt, 2014).

Author and executive director of Missional Intelligence, Mary Lederleitner (2018: 53-54), in her research on women in mission leadership, described the "Faithful Connected Leader" as having the following traits:

- a foundational belief that leadership is not about them but about God and obedience to him (thereby seeing power as also belonging to God);
- a deep commitment to prayer (for transformation and discernment);
- a preference for collaborative leadership;
- a holistic view of mission;
- wise perseverance despite difficulties and injustice;
- intense concern for and monitoring of ministry impact (at organisational, project, and personal levels);
- a commitment to excellence with intentionality concerning ongoing personal growth and development.

Leadership consultant Todd Poulter talks about leadership as "a continual act of worship, carried out at the feet of Jesus with a humbling, attentive, learning, responsive, and corrective posture" (2022: 123-125). Other valuable ideas and practices for leadership are found in writings on servant leadership (Greenleaf, 1998; Trompenaars & Voerman, 2009), steward leadership (Block, 2013; Rodin, 2010; Wilson, 2016; Brinckerhoff, 2004), and shepherd leadership (Laniak, 2006). Henry Nouwen's leadership classic, *In the Name of Jesus* (1992), also offers timeless advice. There are other works available on a wide range of leadership qualities – humility, adaptability, ethics, spirituality. Some are approached from a Christian perspective; others are open to a wide range of belief systems.

There is not nearly as much written on following as on leading, although the body of work on followership is growing. The works mentioned above, however, plus stories such as those of the Lewis and Clark expedition, offer insights for both following and leading. Early church fathers and many Puritan preachers also have much wisdom on what it means to be on a journey with God. Jonathan Edwards wrote a sermon in 1733 entitled, *The Christian Pilgrim; or The True Christian's Life A Journey Toward Heaven.* He ends this instructive message with encouragement to travel in community:

> There are many ways whereby Christians might greatly forward one another in their way to heaven, as by religious conference, etc. Therefore let them be exhorted to go this journey as it were in company: conversing together, and assisting one another. Company is very desirable in a journey, but in none so much as this. — Let them go united and not fall out by the way, which would be to hinder one another, but use all means they can to help each other up the hill. — This would ensure a more successful travelling and a more joyful meeting at their Father's house in glory.

Edwards' sermon is just one example of the wisdom to be found in exploring Puritan thought on the concept of journey.

Most importantly, as we saw in chapter 5, examples from Scripture provide essential guidance for all who are on the journey.

Reviewing some of the literature referred to, four key points come to mind as critical for developing a journey leadership mindset.

> Knowing God – through his Word, through prayer, and through observing his world. It is a necessity and a privilege to know our leader. We need not and cannot know everything he knows, but if we continue to grow in our knowledge of him and our relationship with him, we will flourish as followers and leaders.
>
> Leading through values – integrity, commitment, humility, love. Biblical values are our compass, keeping us true. These are the things that give us stability, roots. Roots that are meant to spread. Don't worry, trees and journeys are not at odds metaphorically; there is evidence of their compatibility in nature and in Tolkien's imaginative depiction of the Ents, the noble, majestic, tree-like shepherds of the trees (2002: 476).
>
> Leading in community – in friendship, through deepening relationships, participating in a local church and the Church worldwide, relying on one another's gifts and wisdom. We are meant to travel together. God intended for the body to live, serve, and worship in unity.
>
> Leading with discernment – when engaged in the three points above, it becomes possible to observe, listen, reflect, and discover what God intends for us and our organisations. Discerning missional intent provides clarity concerning what we can learn from the past, where we are today, and where we are going in the future. Discernment points out the pathway of our journey.

More research and reflection need to take place concerning each of these points in relation to journey. Knowing God takes priority because nothing else will come together without an ongoing relationship with God wherein one is growing in knowledge and wisdom. But it is perhaps the issue of discernment that needs the most attention in terms of further research. How can an organisation, a community, discern together on an ongoing basis as they journey together? As Niemandt reflects, discernment can lead to new learning about ourselves and God, "but demands prophetic courage" (2019a: 113). What does that prophetic courage look like?

How can a journey mentality impact thinking and behaviours regarding key organisational issues?

In the next section, we will address the following question: as a leader, how can a journey mentality impact thinking and behaviours regarding key organisational issues? In the interest of time and space, we have chosen one topic, VUCA, covering various contextual situations. We will look at this one broad topic and then at four related and enduring leadership issues.

If you have been wondering about how to put the journey concept into practice, keep reading!

Leading in a VUCA World

What is VUCA? The US military coined VUCA in the late 1980s to reflect the post-Cold War situation. Yes, it is yet another term that originated with the military. Today, business journals, podcasts, and church consultants offer advice for living in a "VUCA world". The VUCA world is Volatile, Uncertain, Complex, and Ambiguous.

How and why did this term find its way from the US Army College to the desks of non-profit leaders (Tovar, 2016)? From the end of World War II in 1947 to the collapse of the Soviet Union in 1991, a generation of leaders knew the Cold War as their reality, and a generation of youth knew of no other world. Ironically, the Cold War represented a sort of stability, or perhaps familiarity that came to resemble stability. Even when the situation is less than desirable, the semblance of stability represents safety. People long for safety. Safety implies "everything is under control". Ah, and there it is. Control. Safety and control, two highly valued commodities. Putting a VUCA label on the world allows people to name and thereby address a change they struggle to control, or gives them an excuse for not addressing what they see as an unmanageable context (Van Wynen & Niemandt, 2020).

- Feeling Vulnerable, they recognise the world as Volatile;
- feeling Uneasy, they recognise the world as Uncertain;
- feeling Confused, they recognise the world as Complex;
- feeling Anxious, they recognise the world as Ambiguous.

In a *Forbes* article, author and senior fellow at Harvard Business School, Bill George, gives VUCA a positive spin, saying that, to lead in a VUCA world, you need VUCA 2.0: Vision, Understanding, Courage, and Adaptability (George, 2017). In *Harvard Business Review*, Colonel Eric Kail keeps his military stance and language as he writes about fighting VUCA, smashing the four forces, attacking, overcoming. He points out that, even if interconnected, each characteristic requires different tactics and needs to be addressed independently. Kail says, "[Y]ou don't fight VUCA, you fight V, and U, and C, and A. How much do you know about each of these? You need to innovate, be flexible, be prepared, listen more" (Kail, 2011).

Some people say VUCA just stands for, "Hey, it's crazy out there." And there are executives who consider abandoning strategy altogether "because, seriously, how can you plan in such a VUCA world?" (Bennett & Lemoine, 2014).

In an online search for VUCA descriptions and definitions, page after page focused on the fast pace, the turbulence, the world in turmoil, a world so different from past generations. And yet, page after page, professors and pundits quote (usually without giving attribution) the ancient philosopher Heraclitus who, around 500 B.C., stated, "*Panta Rhei*" (Life is flux), usually interpreted and quoted as "the only constant is change" (Britannica, n.d.).

Vision, adaptability, flexibility, listening. This advice for leaders in today's VUCA world doesn't sound like anything new either, which raises the question: when was the world not VUCA? It may be VUCA for different reasons. The main characters and the contexts have changed, but VUCA has always been with us. This does not, however, invalidate the concept. If anything, the concept of ongoing VUCA demonstrates how, deep down, people realise we're on a journey. They might prefer to think of it as a phase, a paradigm, a "whole new ballgame", but to acknowledge VUCA is to acknowledge ongoing change, struggles that are repeated or repackaged through the ages, a level of uncertainty, an inability to predict or control our entire environment. The premise that every era is a VUCA era only reinforces the idea that we are on a journey.

Joubert states, "Leaders urgently need new narratives derived from an entirely new understanding of self, others and reality" (Joubert, 2019: loc 3329). A journey mindset and heart are a possible way forward. The journey concept is helpful in a VUCA context. It can provide freedom from the feeling that the world is spinning out of control, freedom from the compulsion to unceasingly increase speed and innovation. Living within a missiologically sound journey concept means one becomes accustomed to ongoing change and considers it normal. It means God – not jobs, processes, or institutions – is your source of stability. It means you can have optimism in the face of hardship, peace in times of uncertainty, surety even though the future is unknown. It means a quiet walk by the cool waters before facing the next rough VUCA trail. It means that someone far greater than you is in the lead.

Leadership Considerations

The journey concept is applicable in our theological ponderings and in our day-to-day pragmatic pursuits. Rather than looking at some of the current leadership trends and theories (although they are worth looking at from a journey concept perspective), we will briefly explore four critical areas of leadership that are perennial considerations for leaders around the globe. Several of these considerations are also found in, or relate to, VUCA.

The journey and change

My own interest in strategic thinking and leadership began many years ago with a curiosity concerning change. Why are so many people surprised by change? Resistant to change? Suspicious of change? Overwrought or paralysed by change?

Anand and Barsoux's article on change states that, despite the growing knowledge of scholars and consultants, corporate transformations still have a "miserable success rate" (2017: 79). The publication of Bossidy and Charan's book *Execution* in 2009 had executives suddenly focused on execution as the key to overcoming flawed implementation. In a flurry of words and activities bent on regaining control, leaders and managers sought to "carefully manage" change processes, "pull the right levers", and create "burning platforms" to increase pain and thus hasten change (Anand & Barsoux, 2017: 80). Then, they wondered why these efforts (which seem remarkably similar to torture) didn't produce the desired results.

In their efforts to be helpful, change experts may do more harm than good, or inadvertently taint their advice so as to leave negative or misleading impressions. William Bridges' classic and insightful book *Transitions: Making Sense Of Life's Changes* could get readers off to a better start. There are already enough words in the title and enough reason to open the book, without the publisher adding to the cover, "*strategies for coping with the difficult, painful and confusing times in your life*" (Bridges & Bridges, 2019). They have stuck with that tagline, through many editions and cover redesigns, for forty years now. What about the good transitions? Or the changes that may be challenging but also rewarding? Why frame change as something miserable?

Kaufman, an avid sailor, uses a sailing metaphor and the concept of a voyage in his book *Navigating the Winds of Change*. However, amidst all the tremendously helpful advice, he tells his readers to put a plan together for "those items that you have full or partial control over" (Kaufman, 2002: 41). So, what disappointment ensues when the winds of change wrest those items from your hands? Leadership books commonly talk about control, but it might serve better and be more realistic to talk about responsibility rather than control. Responsibility relates to stewardship and commitment. Control assumes power that may be fleeting or fictitious.

Leadership expert John Kotter advises an eight-step process for initiating change (1996: 21). Identifying a process for change is the standard approach, but (even when authors and strategists include disclaimers) such tidy processes foster the notion that you can plan out each step. There may be processes to carry out within the change, but change itself is not predictable and is more complex than a step-by-step process. Bridges offers a transition model that has a "neutral zone" between A (what was) and B (desired future) (1991: 35). While this concept may help people deal with some of the messiness of change, it may also give false expectations that "everything settles down again once we get to B". These are just two of the many theories of transition and change, many of which have been propagated for decades and are still common in change literature and among change consultants.

More recent research focuses on types of change: continuous, disruptive, incremental, etc. Search the internet and you'll find many "definitive" lists of the three, five, six, seven, twelve kinds of change. There are strategies for "managing" each of them. Many of these tools are helpful, but with all this knowledge and all these writings, case studies, and experiments out there, why is there still such resistance to change? And why do people still think they can "manage" change? Peter Bernstein notes, "The past seldom obliges by revealing to us what wildness will break out in the future" (1996: 334). You may have fine-tuned your sports car to perfection, but as you stand on the banks of a wild, raging river, you will realise that your gleaming red vehicle will never get you through the rapids. Weather changes, terrain changes, cultures and contexts change. It's a journey.

Kegan and Lahey (2009: 49) note, "It is not change that causes anxiety; it is the feeling that we are without defences in the presence of what we see as danger". Resistance to change is often a misdiagnosis. Anxiety concerning the unknown could be the real problem. The change itself, or even change in general, may be welcome or at least accepted once a few questions are answered, rumours are put to rest, and the vision for the change is made clearer. When we are in journey-thinking mode, this is apparent. The survey participants had no trouble identifying these same factors and recognising that they were a normal part of the journey.

Resistance to change is closely linked to the desire for safety. While VUCA may have existed for centuries, we are in an age of unprecedented concern for safety and for risk avoidance. According to CEB, a Washington-based firm that researches best practices among its 10,000 member companies, there is excessive focus on preventing risk. In their research of corporate strategy offices, sixty percent cited that focus on risk aversion is causing their company to take too much time to make decisions (HBR, 2015: 20). While the concern noted here was regarding the reduced speed of decision-making, it could as easily apply to the process of making the best decision. Avoiding risk may or may not be the best deciding factor, but it should not be the only factor.

Harvard Business Review's 2018 issue on curiosity defines curiosity as "a penchant for seeking new experiences, knowledge and feedback and an openness to change" (Fernandez-Araoz, Roscoe & Aramaki 2018: 61). Studies show that curiosity is linked to fewer decision errors, more innovation, positive change, open communication, and better team performance. Curiosity leads to creativity which leads to problem-solving, which leads to change. Leaders less likely to pursue curiosity often fear the costs of exploration, the mess, and perceived delays in decision-making. They value efficiency over the possibilities of exploration (Gino, 2018: 52), again avoiding risk.

> *Curiosity leads to creativity which leads to problem-solving, which leads to change.*

Resistance to change, obsession with safety, risk aversion, change management. How is all this affected when you have a journey mindset? First, on a journey, change is expected. Change is ongoing. Change is the norm. It is not an event, or even a series of events. It is life. And it is not managed; it is lived. It will bring challenges, rewards, surprises, disappointments, wisdom. You are better equipped to take on a surprising challenge if the fundamental factor of change itself is not a surprise. You may not expect your kitchen to suddenly sprout boulders, but you are not surprised upon encountering boulders on a hiking trail. The unexpected is expected when you are on a journey. The terrain, weather, and view will change.

Understanding journey as our reality gets even better when we acknowledge God as our leader. There is no change for which he is not ready. God is never surprised, taken off guard, or unprepared.

> Of old you laid the foundation of the earth, and the heavens are the work of your hands. They will perish, but you will remain; they will all wear out like a garment. You will change them like a robe, and they will pass away, but you are the same, and your years have no end. The children of your servants shall dwell secure; their offspring shall be established before you (Ps. 102:25-28).

The journey and complexity

> *Complexity is one of the reasons change may be needed, and change often increases complexity.*

Change and complexity are often mentioned in the same breath. Complexity is one of the reasons change may be needed, and change often increases complexity. Complexity is a quality of VUCA that sends leaders scrambling to restructure and develop resources (Bennett & Lemoine, 2014) to cope with this heavyweight chunk of reality. Complexity is described as the increasing interconnectedness and density of networks – technical processes, tools, systems, infrastructures, products, services, relationships – often all operating on a globally distributed, yet locally controlled, basis.

How-to articles and books abound on reducing, coping with, managing, eliminating, or conquering complexity. In his book *It's Not Complicated*, Nason points out that people often confuse complicated with complex. He deftly explains the difference and warns against approaching the complex with solutions suited for the merely complicated. He states that complicated problems may be hard to solve but can be addressed with rules, systems, and processes. Complex situations, however, involve too many unknowns and interrelated factors to reduce to rules and processes (Nason, 2017). Some leaders and managers address complexity with tools suited for a different era or environment, for a complicated, but not complex, context, or they may choose to ignore the reality of the complexity.

In the article "Managing Yourself to Embrace Complex Change", Brimm describes navigating the seven Cs – complexity, clarity, confidence, creativity, commitment, consolidation, and change. He identifies those who navigate best as "masters of change, global cosmopolitans, highly educated, multilingual, and have lived and worked for extended periods in other cultures. They tend to see change as normal." The author continues, "[T]he trick is to balance this all with some degree of stability in identity, relationship and career" (Brimm, 2015: 112).

- What advantages do Christ-following leaders have in relation to "stability in identity, relationship and career"? How does this help you become a better leader? How could this help you in mentoring others?

Not everyone sees leaders as adept at that balancing act. Author Marilynne Robinson recalls the "old arts of civilisation": religion, politics, philosophy, and music. She then reflects on the modern world picture:

> Economics, the great model among us now, indulges and deprives, builds and abandons, threatens and promises. Its imperium is manifest, irrefragable – as, in fact, it has been since antiquity. Yet suddenly we act as if the reality of economics were reality itself, the one Truth to which everything must refer. I can only suggest that terror at complexity has driven us back to this very crude monism. We have reached a point where cosmology permits us to say that everything might in fact be made of nothing, so we cling to the idea that something is real and necessary, and we have chosen, oddly enough, competition and market forces, taking refuge from the wild epic of cosmic ontogeny by hiding our head in a ledger (1998: 4).

Robinson's phrase "terror at complexity" sounds melodramatic, but only a feeling as strong as terror could drive entire civilisations to become so narrowly focused. This brings to mind another example of oversimplification. In the interest of cleaning up the oceans, people worldwide have been going after the pollution cause which accounts for 0.025 percent of the plastic waste in our waters: plastic straws (Lowrie, 2019). Proponents state that it's low-hanging fruit, something doable, and claim it will draw attention to the more significant issues. However, others fear "banning straws may confer 'moral license' – allowing companies and their customers to feel they have done their part", according to Jim Leape, co-director, Stanford Center for Ocean Solutions (Jordan, 2018). Thinking about economics is not a bad thing. It is just not the only thing. Nor is banning plastic straws a bad thing, but it is a remarkably small part of a large and complex problem. Yet straws remain a focal point.

Complexity is sometimes ignored or misinterpreted, as noted above, but has also, in some quarters, been given great attention. Complexity theory, birthed in the world of computer science, spread to the world of natural sciences, and then to management and organisational studies. Complexity theory is an interdisciplinary theory that grew out of systems theory in the 1960s. It focuses on complex systems with numerous interacting parts, which often give rise to unexpected order. It also relates to chaos theory, which seeks an understanding of simple systems that may change in sudden, unexpected, or irregular ways. The study of complexity and chaos theories in the field of strategic management and organisational studies has led to new perspectives on self-organisation, the nonlinear nature of the world, and the idea of "a natural state between order and chaos, a grand compromise between structure and surprise" (Berreby, 1996: 8). This "natural state" sounds as if it could be describing a journey.

Straub notes that complexity theory has not, however, drastically changed how organisations do business. Although enamoured with complexity theory's "butterfly effect" (the idea that a butterfly flapping its wings in one place can cause changes on the other side of the world), control-focused managers found actual complexity "inconvenient". Straub also mentions that when complexity theory became popular in the 1980s and 90s, technology was not yet powerful enough to capture much complexity. Only in the twenty-first century has computing power and progress in mathematics and statistics made enough headway for the theory to be implemented. Straub notes that many leaders have expressed concern about the eager futurists who talk about machines taking over decision-making and evaluation of contexts and situations but who might overlook the fact that sense-making is always informed by values (Straub, 2013). This dialogue is escalating rapidly as artificial intelligence (AI) has taken huge leaps forward in recent years.

Our lives, our journeys, cannot be reduced to a programmed system any more than they can be reduced to a production line. There is no code, no list of steps. There is no roadmap. But it is possible to embrace complexity from a missional, journey-focused perspective. There is most likely a more natural acceptance of complexity. Journeys, by nature, are complex. Every day, decisions must be made depending on the desired destination, terrain, weather, tools needed, preparedness, and those who travel with you. Relationships are a key factor. The relationships in a missional journey begin, as expected, with God. Once again, surety comes with knowing God is in charge. He will neither ignore, nor be confounded by, complexity. He is the author of complexity, yet is, in himself, simple (Bavinck, 2004: 173-177). Just as he is the unchanging God in a changing world, in his aseity (sufficiency in himself) and simplicity, he is the Creator of all things. His creation is beautifully complex and he comprehends it fully (Barrett, 2019: 71-88).

> God hath all life, glory, goodness, blessedness, in and of himself; and is alone in and unto himself all-sufficient, not standing in need of any creatures which he hath made, nor deriving any glory from them, but only manifesting his own glory in, by, unto, and upon them [...]. To him is due from angels and men, and every other creature, whatsoever worship, service, or obedience he is pleased to require of them (Westminster Confession of Faith [The Westminster Assembly, 1647]).

"The nature of God is simple and immutable and undisturbed, nor is he himself one thing and what he is and has another thing" (Augustine, 1887).

In light of who God is, we can trust complexity to him, the Author of all things. How does this impact how we think and go about our work, our ministry, our participation in his mission? Ongoing prayer is a good start – prayer for clarity, for discernment. God, as our leader, will guide in and through the complexity so we can view it, not as a tangle of threads, but as his beautifully created weaving. As we look closely, we will begin to see the patterns and paths he lays out for us.

The journey and urgency

Urgency. What is it? And how is it expressed? Is it about creating a "burning platform" to increase pain and stress so people are willing to change? Is it needing to respond to a political crisis? Or is it needing to get the numbers up for the next stakeholders' meeting? Is it about providing emergency healthcare, social justice, saving endangered species or the planet? In the church and Christian non-profit sectors, is it an urgency to share the gospel with those who do not believe or who have not heard? Is it urgency to complete specific tasks or projects related to organisational mandates? Or is it a desire to be more relevant, better equipped, or more prominent than the church down the street? Or, perhaps, the urgency is just to pay the bills.

The corporate world, as well as the Christian community, seems torn on the subject of urgency. For decades, the theme has been about creating a sense of urgency. Kotter recalls that, while writing the fable *Our Iceberg is Melting*, he was frequently asked, "What is the single biggest error people make when they try to change?" (2008: 49). (Yes, change, complexity, and urgency are all connected.) Kotter responded, after reflection, that the error is the failure to create a high enough sense of urgency among enough people to set the stage for the challenging leap in some new direction (2008: 49). He warns against both complacency and false urgency (identified by frenzied activity driven by anxiety, anger, and frustration) and notes the increasing urgency of urgency, citing the shift in change from episodic to continuous. This shift speaks to the other side of the urgency issue in the corporate world.

Most corporations today are not finding it necessary to create a crisis in order to create a mandate for change. VUCA, the endless drive for innovation, political and social shifts, the movement from institutions and jobs once thought stable, secure, and sustainable to agile companies and free agents (who are only free as far as their self-promotion and bank accounts will take them) are among the many forces that drive a sense of urgency. According to Kok and van den Heuvel, "Many would agree we live in one of the fastest changing times in history and that the change we experience now might be just as large and significant as the change between the Middle Ages and the modern world […]. [W]e are overflooded with incoming streams of communication" (2019: loc 25). On the other hand, Nonaka and Zhu remind us that other experts have warned against the arrogance of thinking that we face unprecedented change, or that we need or can find quick solutions to management challenges that have existed for ages (2012: 12).

Historian Ian Mortimer, responding to the question, "Which century saw the most change?", is quick to point out that all of the changes cited for the twentieth century (and it would apply to the twenty-first thus far, as well) were primarily technological. He then reminds the reader of the many changes through the ages that were not technological (2014). However, did that make those ages any less VUCA, or did people have a lesser sense of urgency? The rise of feudalism, the growth of markets and spread of money in the Middle Ages, The Black Death, the discoveries of Columbus and other explorers, human rights revolutions. These changes and events must have triggered or been triggered by a sense of urgency somewhere.

We must discern where the true and false urgencies lie. What's worth urgency? Why? How will that urgency be turned into action? The many and varied responses to COVID-19 provide a good case study of the complexity that comes when there are varying viewpoints on both urgency and priorities. There is no simple answer, no formula for success.

In 2016, the Wycliffe Global Alliance held its quadrennial Global Gathering. More than 100 organisational leaders and board representatives gathered to connect, worship, and discuss key issues. One of the discussions was on urgency. They were asked, as table groups, to reflect on the theme of urgency as it related to Vision 2025 (a commitment made in the late 1990s by Wycliffe and one of its partner organisations, SIL, to demonstrate willingness to think and work differently with a goal of seeing translation started by 2025 in every language community that needed it). The following are a few of the comments worth further reflection:

- A right attitude toward urgency never harms community.
- Justice motivates us toward urgency.
- Jesus was always busy, but never in a hurry. He always had time to pray.
- Urgency is following the urging of the Holy Spirit with prayer and patience.
- Healthy urgency requires a parallel process of reflection.
- Our scale of urgency is measured by how we understand God's mind, his will, his methods, and how he will use us.
- God's patience calls for a sense of urgency.
- Urgency is about stewardship of the resources and abilities God has given us for his mission.
- Urgency is purposefulness/intentionality.
- Coordinate, collaborate, share, work interdependently.
- Urgency drives us toward creative solutions.
- We must have an urgency to BE before the DO.
- It's essential to have a sense of God's timing.
- Urgency to reach a deadline is less compelling than urgency toward a preferred future (Global Gathering, 2016).

It is worth noting how even the theme of urgency comes back to prayer, discernment, community, stewardship. These are grounding elements of life in Christ, of our journey with him. Any call to urgency is actually a call to obedience. Whatever the causes, issues, or needs, our urgency must always be to

> *Whatever the causes, issues, or needs, our urgency must always be to obey.*

obey. God will orchestrate the priorities, provisions, and plans as we seek to discern and obey.

God knows all things past, present, and future. He is not bound by time. "His knowledge is primary, always preceding who we are and what we know" (Barrett, 2019: 194). So, he does not relate to urgency in the same sense that we do, but he can speak into our time-bound lives and impress upon us an urgency to obedience.

The journey and success

In the corporate world, success traditionally means "winning", being the best. It could mean having the best product, service, or earnings. It could even extend to having the best employee benefits, if the other points above are successfully implemented first. Alternatively, it could mean "winning" by having the most – the most customers, money, power. Perhaps it's about capturing a niche market. In recent years, it also includes having the most seductive product, and then another, and another, and another. All this while "building" the case for why potential customers can't live without the product.

Management professor Rita Gunther McGrath states that the goal of sustainable, competitive advantage now often needs to be replaced by transient advantage goals (2013: loc 2443). Reflecting on the former economy, McGrath stated, "Today that way of thinking about strategy is in tatters. It would be easy to bemoan the loss of so much security and stability" (2013: loc 2708). However, she goes on to talk about the new opportunities for creativity, the greater variety of options.

It's apparent that at least some of the definitions of success are changing. Having a stable, sustainable company was once a model of success, but today's picture of success is of the ever-innovating, transient opportunist. More companies and organisations, however, are seeing advantages to co-operation and not just competition. That is a by-product of complexity. Many companies also add social consciousness and activities to their list of successes (although that is not as new as some might think if you look into the history of companies such as Cadbury and others that were founded on moral as well as capitalistic principles [Cadbury, 2010: 93]).

Another measure of success is learning. Peter Senge popularised learning organisations and systems thinking in his 1990 book *The Fifth Discipline* (Senge, 1990). Nonaka and Takeuchi (1995) promoted a similar idea in their work on knowledge-creating companies. They all encouraged ongoing learning as a way of being, not just as a specialised activity. However, for many organisations, the idea never got off the bookshelf.

"Why organisations don't learn" was a topic of research conducted over a ten-year period and released in 2015. "Too much focus on success" was cited as one of the top roadblocks to organisational learning. Organisations tend to act too quickly, relying too much on past performance. The authors noted that people credit brilliance and skill to past successes, but consider failure as just "bad fortune". They don't take time to reflect or to learn (Gino & Staats, 2015: 111). Ironically, if these organisations had incorporated learning into their measures of success, they would have appeared to be more successful.

At the core, however, most business success stories are still about money, acquisition, power. These are not, however, kingdom ministry goals for missional journey leaders. Progress and success take on new meanings when participating in God's mission. As stated before, it is his mission, and he is in charge. Therefore, any progress, any success, is by his hand and is defined by him. Why do so many persist in valuing and measuring their success, progress, and effectiveness by standards that should not apply? Expectations and perceived expectations play a significant role.

Obedience, love, and unity are all portrayed as measures of success in God's eyes. In John 17, Jesus prays for believers, that they might be one as he and the Father are one. What does success look like in John 17?

- that they may have my joy fulfilled in themselves (v.13);
- that you keep them from the evil one (v.15);
- sanctify them in the truth; your Word is truth (v.17);
- the glory that you have given me I have given to them, that they may be one even as we are one […] so that the world may know that you sent me and loved them even as you loved me (vv.21-23).

Success is God glorified in us and through us as we become one. It has always been about him, not us. The often recited Great Commission passage in Matthew 28 has long drawn followers of Christ into obedience. But so often the focus is on what we should do: go, make disciples, baptise, teach (vv.19-20), and we look at ourselves, chide ourselves, track our "success" rather than look to the One who, in the same breath, said that "[a]ll authority in heaven and on earth" has been given to him and that he will be with us. The success of God's mission, your organisation, or your church is not dependent on you. Your calling is to follow, obey, become more like Christ.

As followers and leaders under God's direction on this journey, that reality should not only be a source of great joy, but also great relief. These are no small responsibilities – to love, be generous, and show mercy – but neither do they call for "success" by the standards we so often set for ourselves. It is only through Christ that we have any measure of success. Sometimes, our greatest learnings are through our greatest failings. C.S. Lewis wrote, "We all want progress. But progress means getting nearer to the place you want to be. And if you have taken a wrong turning, then to go forward does not get you any nearer. If you are on the wrong road, progress means doing an about-turn and walking back to the right road; and in that case the man who turns back soonest is the most progressive man" (1952: 22). We will make mistakes, we will sometimes exercise poor judgment, or experience moral failures. We must distinguish the difference and learn from each. And we must trust God to forgive and, in his own way and timing, to make things right.

Our sanctification is a continuing change God works in us. His strength shines through our weakness. When we falter on the path, he lights the way. God provides, and he does it in so many ways. Look at examples from the Old Testament. He can conquer daunting armies in battle, and he can provide a discouraged man with fresh-baked bread. It is corporate and it is personal. God works in and through individuals and the collective body in configurations that include churches, organisations, families.

Derek Thomas, in his book on the eighth chapter of Romans, states, "They [Christians] learn to live, as the Puritans who encouraged their flocks long ago, *sub specie aeternitatis* 'from the standpoint of eternity' […] with life in this world viewed as a pilgrimage to the next" (2011: 37).

Dietrich Bonhoeffer wrote, "[E]ach moment, lived in God's sight, can bring an unexpected decision. Thus, only one thing can be repeated again and again, also in our time: in ethical decisions, a man must consider his action *sub specie aeternitatis* and then, no matter how it proceeds, it will proceed rightly" (2008: 368).

This is not just "spiritual talk". Yes, it is spiritual, but there is nothing more practical, applicable, or necessary to our journey than spiritual life and direction. We do not withdraw. We fully engage, but we do so fully aware that God's vantage point is far beyond anything we can envision and, yet, he makes the way available to us through his most gracious leading. May we proceed rightly.

Bibliography

Ambrose, S. 1996. *Undaunted Courage.* New York: Touchstone, Simon and Schuster.

Anand, N. and J.L. Barsoux. 2017. "What Everybody Gets Wrong About Change Management." *Harvard Business Review* 11-12 (December): 79-85.

Anderson, I. 1997. "To equip an expedition." *Inside the Corps. PBS.* Premiered: 4th November 1997. [Available at: https://www.pbs.org/lewisandclark/inside/idx_equ.html], [Last accessed: 23th September 2023].

Anonymous. 1936. "Child in The Home." *The New Wonder World.* 11 Vols. Chicago, IL: Geo. L. Shuman & Co.

Anonymous. 1945. *Fifty Famous Fairy Tales.* Racine, WI: Whitman.

Araujo, A., M. Lederleitner, and W. Mischke. 2008. "To Catch the Wind: A New Metaphor for Cross-Cultural Mission Partnerships." *Interchange Postings.* (December 2008) Wheaton, IL: COSIM Conference 2008. [Available at: https://catalystservices.org/wp-content/uploads/2012/08/Wind.pdf], [Last accessed: 23rd September 2023].

Araujo, A. and W. Mischke. 2009. "Catching the Wind of God – A Sailing Retreat." *Sailing Friends Website.* Belhaven College, Jackson, MP: Sailing Friends. [Available at: https://sailingfriends.files.wordpress.com/2009/10/sailboat_retreat_report_15oct20092.pdf], [Last accessed: 23rd September 2023].

Audebrand, L. 2017. "Sustainability in strategic management education: the quest for new root metaphors." *Academy of Management Learning and Education* 9(3), (September 2010). Published online: 30th Nov 2017. [Available at: https://journals.aom.org/doi/10.5465/amle.9.3.zqr413], [Last accessed: 23th September 2023].

Augustine. 1887. *Treatise on the Trinity.* Amazon digital.

Barrett, M. 2019. *None Greater: the undomesticated attributes of God.* Grand Rapids, MI: Baker.

Bavinck, H. 2004. *God and Creation.* Vol. 2 of *Reformed Dogmatics.* Grand Rapids, MI: Baker.

Beaumont, M. 1756. *Beauty and the Beast.* London: Global Grey, 2018. [Available at: https://www.globalgreyebooks.com/beauty-and-the-beast-ebook.html], [Last accessed: 23rd September 2023].

Bennett, N. and G.J. Lemoine. 2014. "What VUCA really means for you." *Harvard Business Review* (Jan-Feb 2014). [Available at: https://hbr.org/2014/09/a-framework-forunderstanding-vuca/], [Last accessed: 23rd September 2023].

Bernstein, P. 1996. *Against the Gods: The Remarkable Story of Risk.* New York: John Wiley & Sons.

Berreby, D. 1996. "Between Chaos and Order: What Complexity Theory Can Teach Business" (online reprint). *Organizations and People* 3(24). [Available at: https://www.strategy-business.com/article/15099?gko=d48d4], [Last accessed: 23rd September 2023].

Block, P. 2013. *Stewardship: Choosing Service Over Self-Interest.* Williston, ND: Berrett-Koehler.

Bonhoeffer, D. 2008. *Barcelona, Berlin, New York 1928-1931.* Vol. 10 of *Dietrich Bonhoeffer Works.* Minneapolis, MN: Fortress.

Bosch, D.J. 1991. *Transforming Mission.* New York: Orbis.

—. 1979. *A Spirituality of the Road.* Eugene, OR: Wipf and Stock.

Bridges, W. 1991. *Managing Transitions*. Reading: Addison-Wesley.

Bridges, W. and S. Bridges. 2019. *Transitions: Making Sense of Life's Changes*. Revised 40th anniversary ed. Boston, MA: Da Capo Lifelong Books.

Brimm, L. 2015. "Managing Yourself: How to Embrace Complex Change." *Harvard Business Review* (September): 108-112. [Available at: https://hbr.org/2015/09/how-to-embrace-complex-change], [Last accessed: 23rd September 2023].

Brinckerhoff, P. 2004. *Nonprofit Stewardship: A Better Way to Lead Your Mission-Based Organization.* Saint Paul, MN: Fieldstone Alliance.

Brooks, D. 2011. "Poetry for everyday life." *New York Times* (11 April, A25). [Available at: https://www.nytimes.com/2011/04/12/opinion/12brooks.html], [Last accessed: 23rd September 2023].

Bryson, J.M. 2004. *Strategic Planning for Public and Nonprofit Organizations.* 3rd ed. San Francisco, CA: Jossey-Bass.

Bunyan, J. 1678. *The Pilgrim's Progress*. public domain.

Cadbury, D. 2010. *Chocolate Wars: the 150 year rivalry between the world's greatest chocolate makers*. Philadelphia, PA: Public Affairs Press.

Capek, T. 1906. *The Slovaks of Hungary, Slavs and Panslavism.* Albany, NY: Knickerbocker Press.

Chesterton, G.K. 1908. *Orthodoxy*. 2023 ed. Louisville, KY: Memoria Press.

Chussil, M. 2016. "'Rally the troops' and other business metaphors you can do without." *Harvard Business Review* (24th November). [Available at: https://hbr.org/2016/11/rally-the-troops-and-other-business-metaphors-you-can-do-without], [Last accessed 23rd September 2023].

Clarke, C. 1970. *The Men of the Lewis and Clark Expedition,* 2002 ed. Lincoln, NE: Bison Books, University of Nebraska.

Couse E., Ed. 1893. *The History of the Lewis and Clarke Expedition.* 3 Vols. Unabridged republication of the four-volume edition published by Francis P. Harper (1893). New York: Dover.

Creswell, J.W., W.E. Hanson, V.L. Clark Plano, and A. Morales. 2007. "Qualitative Research Designs: Selection and Implementation." *The Counseling Psychologist* 35(2): 236-264. [Available at: https://journals.sagepub.com/doi/abs/10.1177/0011000006287390], [Last accessed: 23rd September 2023].

Danker, F. 2000. *A Greek-English Lexicon of the New Testament and Other Early Christian Literature.* 3rd ed. Chicago, IL: University of Chicago Press.

Edwards, J. n.d. The Sermons of Jonathan Edwards (1703-1758). *A Puritan's Mind Website.* [Available at: https://www.apuritansmind.com/puritan-favorites/jonathan-edwards/sermons/the-christian-pilgrim/], [Last accessed: 23rd September 2023].

Ellul, J. 1989. *What I Believe.* Translated by G.W. Bromiley. Grand Rapids, MI: Eerdmans.

Encyclopedia Britannica. n.d. Heraclitus. [Available at: https://www.britannica.com/biography/Heraclitus], [Last accessed: 23rd September 2023].

ESV. 2008. *ESV Study Bible.* Wheaton, IL: Crossway Bibles.

Fairytalez.com website. n.d. [Available at: http://fairytalez.com], [Last accessed: 23rd September 2023].

Faust, A.B. 1920. *Lists of Swiss Emigrants in the Eighteenth Century to the American Colonies.* Vol. 1. Washington DC: National Genealogical Society.

Fernandez-Araoz, A., A. Roscoe, and K. Aramaki. 2018. "From Curious to Competent." *Harvard Business Review* (Sept-Oct): 61.

Francis, J.A. "One Solitary Life". On *Tullylish Parish Website.* [Available at: http://www.tullylish.com/christmas/85-reflections], [Last accessed: 23rd September 2023].

Franklin, K. 2017. *Towards Global Missional Leadership.* Oxford: Regnum.

Franklin, K. and S. van Wynen. 2022. *A Missional Leadership History.* Oxford: Regnum.

Freedman, L. 2013. *Strategy: A History.* New York: Oxford University Press.

Frost, R. 1931. "Education by Poetry." *Amherst Graduates Quarterly* (February 1931). [Available at: http://moodyap.pbworks.com/f/frost.EducationByPoetry.pdf], [Last accessed: 23rd September 2023].

Gaddis, J.L. 2018. *On Grand Strategy.* New York: Penguin Press.

Geary, J. 2011. *I is an Other: The Secret Life of Metaphor and How It Shapes the Way We See the World.* New York: HarperCollins ebooks.

George, B. 2017. "*VUCA 2.0:* a strategy for steady leadership in an unsteady world."

Forbes (17th February 2017). [Available at: https://www.forbes.com/sites/hbsworkingknowledge/2017/02/17/vuca-2-0-a-strategy-for-steady-leadership-in-an-unsteady-world/#4d9a41cc13d8], [Last accessed: 23rd September 2023].

George, T. 2011. *Reading Scripture with the Reformers.* Downers Grove, IL: InterVarsity Press.

Gino, F. and B. Staats. 2015. "Why organizations don't learn." *Harvard Business Review* 93(11): 110-118.

Gino, F. 2018. "The business case for curiosity". *Harvard Business Review* (Sept-Oct): 48-57.

Greenia, G. 2018. "What is Pilgrimage?" *International Journal of Religious Tourism and Pilgrimage* 6(2): 7-15.

Greenleaf, R.K. 1998. *The Power of Servant-Leadership*. San Francisco, CA: Berrett-Koehler.

Greenwald, J. and B. Kahn. 2005. *Competition Demystified: A Radically Simplified Approach to Business Strategy*. London: Penguin.

Grimm, J. and W. Grimm. n.d. *The Musicians of Brementown.* 19th-Century German Stories on the Virginia Commonwealth University website. [Available at: https://archive.vcu.edu/germanstories/grimm/bremereng.html], [Last accessed: 23rd September 2023].

Hargis, M. 1998. "On the Road: the inns and outs of travel in first-century Palestine." [Available at: https://www.christianitytoday.com/history/issues/issue-59/on-road.html], [Last accessed: 23rd September 2023].

Hart, J. 2007. *A Writer's Coach.* New York: Anchor.

Hauerwas, S. and W.H. Wilimon. 2014. *Resident Aliens: Life in the Christian Colony,* 25th anniversary ed. Nashville, TN: Abingdon Press.

Havel, V. 1990. *New Year's Address to the Nation.* [Available at: http://old.hrad.cz/president/Havel/speeches/1990/0101_uk.html], [Last accessed: 23rd September 2023].

HBR, Eds. 2015. "Strategy – how to live with risks." *Harvard Business Review* (July-August 2015): 20.

Hofmeyr, I. 2004. *The Portable Bunyan: A Transnational History of The Pilgrim's Progress.* Princeton: Princeton University Press.

Homer. 800 BCE. *The Iliad.* Trans. by Samuel Butler [Available at: http://classics.mit.edu/Homer/iliad.1.i.html], [Last accessed: 23rd September 2023].

Ibsen, H. 2003. *Peer Gynt.* Replication of 1875 translated ed. Mineola, NY: Dover.

Jordan, R. 2018. "Do plastic straws really make a difference?" *Stanford Earth* (8th September 2018). [Available at: https://earth.stanford.edu/news/do-plastic-straws-really-make-difference], [Last accessed: 23rd September 2023].

Joubert, S. 2019. "A well-played life: discernment as the constitutive building block of selfless leadership." In J. Kok and S. van den Heuvel, Eds. *Leading in a VUCA World: integrating leadership, discernment and spirituality.* (loc 3284-3553) Cham, Germany: Springer.

Kail, E. 2010. "Leading effectively in a VUCA environment." *Harvard Business Review* 3rd November 2010. [Available at:

https://hbr.org/2010/11/leading-in-a-vuca-environment.html], [Last accessed: 23rd September 2023].

Kaufman, A. 2002. *Navigating the Winds of Change: Staying On Course in Business & In Life.* Tallahassee, FL: Zurich Press.

Kegan, R. and L.L. Lahey. 2009. *Immunity to Change.* Boston, MA: Harvard Business Review Press.

Keifert, P. 2006. *We Are Here Now: a new missional era, a missionary journey of Spiritual Discovery.* Eagle, ID: Allelon.

Kimbi, P. 2018. "Brief historical origins of the Kom people." Unpublished.

Kok, J. and S. van den Heuvel. 2019. *Leading in a VUCA World: integrating leadership, discernment and spirituality.* Cham, Germany: Springer.

Kotter, J.P. 2008. *A Sense of Urgency.* Boston, MA: Harvard Business School Press.

—. 1996. *Leading Change.* Boston, MA: Harvard Business School Press.

Kovecses, Z. 2015. *Where Metaphors Come From: Reconsidering Context in Metaphor.* New York: Oxford University Press.

Koyama, K. 1979. *Three Mile an Hour God.* Maryknoll, NY: Orbis Books.

Laniak, T.S. 2006. *Shepherds After My Own Heart: Pastoral Traditions and Leadership in the Bible.* Downers Grove, IL: IVP Academic.

Lawley, J. and P. Tompkins. 2013. *Metaphors in Mind.* Carmarthen: Crown House.

Lederleitner, M. 2019. *Women in God's Mission: Accepting the Invitation to Serve and Lead.* Downers Grove, IL: InterVarsity.

Lendvai, P. 2004. *The Hungarians: A Thousand Years of Victory in Defeat.* Princeton, NJ: Princeton University Press.

Levinson, J.C. 2007. *Guerilla Marketing.* 4th ed. New York: Houghton Mifflin.

Lewis, C.S. 1939. "Bluspels and Flalansferes: A Semantic Nightmare". In W. Hooper, Ed. *Selected Literary Essays.* Cambridge University Press.

—. 1952. *Mere Christianity.* New York: Macmillan.

—. 1970a. *The Magician's Nephew.* New York: Macmillan.

—. 1970b. *Prince Caspian.* New York: Macmillan.

—. 1970c. *The Horse and His Boy.* New York: Macmillan.

—. 1970d. *The Last Battle.* New York: Macmillan.

—. 1970e.*The Silver Chair.* New York: Macmillan.

—. 1970f. *The Voyage of the Dawn Treader.* New York: Macmillan.

—. 1994. *The Lion, The Witch and the Wardrobe.* New York: Harper Collins.

Lowell, J. 1868. James Russell Lowell on Democracy. *Inaugural Address.* [Available at: http://xroads.virginia.edu/~DRBR/lowell2.html], [Last accessed: 23rd September 2023].

Lowrie, A. 2019. "Paper straws won't stop climate change." *The Atlantic* (20th August 2019) [Available at: https://www.theatlantic.com/ideas/archive/2019/08/paper-straws-wont-stop-climate-change/596302/], [Last accessed: 23rd September 2023].

Mason, H. trans. 1970. *Gilgamesh – A Verse Narrative.* New York: Mariner.

McCullough, D. 1984. "Historian Addresses Wesleyan". *New York Times* 3rd June 1984. [Available at:

https://www.nytimes.com/1984/06/04/nyregion/historian-addresses-wesleyan.html], [Last accessed: 23rd September 2023].

McGrath, R.G. 2013. *The End of Competitive Advantage: How to keep your strategy moving as fast as your business*. Boston, MA: Harvard Business Review Press.

Mintzberg, H. 2013. *The Rise and Fall of Strategic Planning*. New York: Free Press.

Mortimer, I. 2014. "What century saw the most change?" *History Extra (BBC)*.
[Available at: https://www.historyextra.com/period/norman/which-century-saw-the-most-change/], [Last accessed: 23rd September 2023].

Nason, R. 2017. *It's Not Complicated: The Art and Science of Complexity in Business*. Toronto: Rotman-UTP.

Nell, M. 2019. "Military Metaphors We Lead By: Paul's self-enactment as a field commander." In S. Jung, V. Kessler, L. Kretzchmar, and E. Meier, Eds. *Metaphors for Leading – Leading by Metaphors.* Göttingen: V&R Unipress. 89-100.

Newbigin, L. 1995. *The Open Secret*. Revised, Grand Rapids, MI: Wm. B. Eerdmans.

Niemandt, C.J.P. 2014. "Developing Missional Congregations." Paper presented at Council for World Mission African Regional Assembly. [Available at: https://www.academia.edu/8028751/Developing_missional_congregations_paper_de%20livered_at_the_Council_for_World_Mission_African_Assembly], [Last accessed: 23rd September 2023].

——. 2019a. *Missional Leadership.* Capetown: AOSIS.

——. 2019b. "'Narraphors' in missional transformation of South African denominations: a herd of buffaloes." In S. Jung, V. Kessler, L. Kretzchmar, and E. Meier, Eds. *Metaphors for Leading – Leading by Metaphors.* Göttingen: V&R Unipress. 187-199.

Nonaka, I. and H. Takeuchi. 1995. *The Knowledge-Creating Company: How Japanese Companies Create the Dynamics of Innovation*. Oxford: Oxford University Press.

Nonaka, I. and Z. Zhu. 2012. *Pragmatic Strategy: Eastern Wisdom, Global Success*. New York: Cambridge University Press.

Nouwen, H. 1992. *In the Name of Jesus*. Chestnut Ridge, NY: The Crossroad Publishing Company.

Oxford English Dictionary. 2023. "Metaphor". *OED*. [Available at: https://www.oed.com/search/dictionary/?scope=Entries&q=metaphor], [Last accessed: 24th September 2023].

Poulter, T. 2022. *Learning to Lead at the Feet of Jesus: Encounters with Grace and Truth.* Pasadena, CA: William Carey.

Ransome, A. 1922. *The Soldier and Death; a Russian folk tale told in English.* Digitised archive book, The Library of Congress. New York: B.W. Huebsch. [Available at: https://archive.org/details/soldierdeathruss00rans/page/n8/mode/2up], [Last accessed: 24th September 2023].

Richards, R. and B. O'Brien. 2012. *Misreading Scripture with Western Eyes: Removing Cultural Blinders to Better Understand the Bible.* Downers Grove, IL: InterVarsity Press.

Robinson, M. 1998. *The Death of Adam.* New York: Picador.

Rodin, S. 2010. *The Steward Leader: Transforming People, Organizations and Communities.* Downers Grove, IL: IVP Academic.

Senge, Peter M. 1990. *The Fifth Discipline: The Art and Practice of the Learning Organization.* New York: Doubleday/Currency.

Simmons, M.W. 2016. *Peter the Great: Autocrat and Reformer.* Scotts Valley, CA: CreateSpace.

Steinbeck, J. 1967. *The Grapes of Wrath.* New York: Viking.

Steiner, G. 1969. *Top Management Planning.* New York: MacMillian.

Stern, R., Ed. 1946. *Book Trails,* Vol. 7. Chicago: Child Development.

Straub, R. 2013. "Why managers haven't embraced complexity." *Harvard Business Review* 6th May 2013. [Available at: https://hbr.org/2013/05/why-managers-havent-embraced-c], [Last accessed: 24th September 2023].

Strong, J. 2009. *Strong's Exhaustive Concordance.* Peabody, MA: Hendrickson.

Sweet, L. 2015. *From Tablet to Table.* Colorado Springs, CO: NavPress.

Tennent, T. 2010. *Invitation to World Missions: A Trinitarian Missiology for the 21st Century.* Grand Rapids, MI: Kregel Academic.

Terry, J.M. and J.D. Payne. 2013. *Developing a Strategy for Missions.* Grand Rapids, MI: Baker Academics.

Thomas, D.H.W. 2011. *How the Gospel Brings Us All the Way Home.* Lake Mary, FL: Reformation Trust.

Tolkien, J.R.R. 1966. *The Hobbit.* New York: Ballantine.

——. 2002. *Lord of the Rings,* 50th anniversary edn. New York: Houghton Mifflin.

Tovar, P. 2016. "Leadership challenges in the V.U.C.A. world." *Oxford Leadership.* [Available at: https://www.oxfordleadership.com/leadership-challenges-in-the-v-u-c-a-world/], [Last accessed: 24th September 2023].

Trompenaars, F. and E. Voerman. 2009. *Servant-Leadership Across Cultures: Harnessing the Strengths of the World's Most Powerful Management Philosophy.* New York: McGraw Hill Education.

Van Wynen, S.E. 2009. "From Monocultural to Intercultural." Master's thesis, Azusa Pacific University.

Verne, J. 2005. *Journey to the Center of the Earth.* Oxford: Oxford University Press.

Westminster Assembly. 1647. "The 1647 Westminster Confession of Faith." *A Puritan's Mind Website.* [Available at: www.apuritansmind.com/westminster-standards/chapter-2/], [Last accessed: 24th September 2023].

Wilson, K. 2016. *Steward Leadership in the Nonprofit Organization.* Downers Grove, IL: InterVarsity Press.

Wright, C.J.H. 2006. *The Mission of God.* Downers Grove, IL: InterVarsity Press Academic.

Wycliffe Global Alliance. 2016. Global Gathering 2016. Paper compiled from conference participant discussions.

Appendix

Wait a few minutes, our lantern will be lit, and, if you like light places, you will be satisfied.

Jules Verne, Twenty Thousand Leagues Under the Sea

On the Road – Practical Applications of the Journey Concept

Perhaps you are already planning to walk through this book with your team or colleagues. You may already have ideas for approaching the questions offered in the book, or are eager to implement some of the principles. You may already be discerning how you will proceed on your journey.

Or perhaps you are just about ready to set the book aside and get back to doing things the way you've always done them because that's what you know. But wait!

This appendix offers practical examples and ideas for putting the journey concept into practice. So, let's light the lantern and move forward.

Journey overview

1. We are on a journey. As we have established:

- The journey is both literal and figurative. Our journey is our ongoing participation with God in his mission, at his invitation, under his direction, for his glory.
- We were not given a task to do *for* God. He has invited us to come *with* him. He has called us to join him, to follow him.
- We do not need to set our own agenda, chart our own course, or determine our own destiny. We do need to pray, discern, and obey the God we follow.
- We need to be accountable, serve in community, and be good stewards of what God has given us.
- There is no roadmap. We've never been this way before. But we are not alone.

> - How does this perspective help you think differently about your role and responsibilities? How does it help you think differently about strategy and planning?

2. Identity and missional intent. As we participate in God's mission, we see our identity as connected to God's purposes.

- Our identity is found in God and his purposes, and is fulfilled as we glorify him.
- We encourage and practice community, friendship, generosity.
- We follow Christ. As he guides and directs, we discern what our part in God's mission might look like. This is an ongoing process.
- We commit our hearts and minds to specific areas of focus. This is our Missional Intent.

If you are an organisation, church, or team leader, your vision, mission, purpose, and values shape your missional intent. Your organisation should already have a:

- Vision (the future you desire to see. *Why* your organisation exists).
- Mission (the specific nature of your participation in God's mission. *What* you do to move toward your vision).
- Purpose (declares *who* you are in relation to others. Sometimes it is a part of your Mission statement. It's the big picture of *how* you fulfil your mission)

- Take time to review your Vision, Mission, and Purpose. If you haven't done this recently, you will also want to address the questions of *who* is involved, *where* you serve (your scope of influence), and any timeframes to which you are subject (the *whens*).

3. The Journey Concept. This is not a five-year plan, a scorecard, or an output-based planning model. Many of these approaches can be helpful in project management, but they are not robust enough for leadership or for navigating the complex contexts leaders face today. Nor do they have a missiological or theological basis on which to build. What makes the Journey Concept different? It's real. We do it together. It's not static; it's in motion. It's about both following and leading.

With this understanding, we realise we also need a different way to think about, talk about, process, and practice strategy and planning. We need to be grounded in who God is and where he's going.

- Recommended: an ongoing group Bible study reflecting on who God is, his character, the names of God, the actions of God, etc.
- Recommended: an ongoing group Bible study reflecting on what God is doing in and for the world. How is his mission evident in his Word?

Planning for the ongoing journey

Aligning our thinking with God's mission requires rethinking. As you have probably realised by now, managing change and getting through a "transition zone" isn't the most realistic approach. Unlike what has often been presented in leadership and management training in the past, the journey doesn't end when we get from point A to point B. We live in the nebulous zone. We are pilgrims, sojourners, and often explorers.

You can learn to navigate change, but "managing" it would be like managing the waves of the ocean. We mislead our colleagues if we assure them "things will settle down". Change becomes part of the day-to-day landscape if you have a journey mindset. You expect change and are less fearful of change. You can't prepare for everything, but even when you don't know what's next, you can prepare for some things. And you have the constant reminder and encouragement that God is in charge.

- What evidence do you see that the old ways of working aren't working?
- How can you help your team develop a journey mentality? The exercises below can help.

Journey elements

Start with basic questions, and enjoy a casual discussion as a team (or perhaps start with a few members of your team). Allow plenty of time. You may want to take several days or have sessions once a week for a designated stretch of time. Then take time individually and as a team to reflect deeply on your options and responses. Be sure to take good notes!

We are on a journey:

- Who are we following?
- Where are we going? Why?
- How do we get there?
- What skills and gifts are needed?
- Who is travelling with us?
- What is needed for their (and our) well-being? (Consider such things as health, balance, and growth: spiritual, physical, mental, emotional, relational, meaningful purpose.)
- What is our context?
    - Climate
    - Weather
    - Terrain
- What resources do we have?
- What resources do we need?
- What is important to hold on to? To let go of or to leave behind?
- Are we prepared for change?
- What might help us prepare?

- What might need to change in our thinking and structures?
- How do we describe the following in our organisation? How might these need to change?
    - Progress;
    - Effectiveness;
    - Value of speed (faster, cheaper, no loss of quality);
    - Impact;
    - Efficiency;
    - Short-term, long-term impact;
    - Sustainability;
    - Return on investment;
    - Success;
    - Urgency.

This exercise, once evaluated, should enable your team to have robust discussions, times of discernment, and the ability to figure out next steps. It is an organic process and will look different for each team and organisation.

Journey examples

This section provides examples of teams that put the journey concept into practice. Each example also includes practical application points you can use with your team.

LEADERS PREPARE FOR WHAT'S NEXT

My first opportunity to explore the journey concept was with a group of African colleagues over a decade ago. It was a strategic planning workshop. Some participants were leaders of national organisations, and some were communication or personnel directors. They were enthusiastic about the chance to be together, learn from each other, and, perhaps, make progress with strategic planning for their organisations. We took time to get acquainted (many of them already knew each other) and talked about hopes, expectations, and fears. I asked them if they had done organisation planning using tools such as SWOT (Strengths, Weaknesses, Opportunities, Threats), scenario planning, scorecards, frameworks, and RBM (Results Based Management) and if they had used terms such as input, output, outcomes, etc. There were groans.

One participant spoke up quickly. "I think our problem is, perhaps, that English is not our first language." Others nodded. I agreed that this could be a factor, but told them that many native English speakers find these tools and methodologies frustrating as well. Some are overly complex; others are suited for project management but not for leading an organisation. Some were designed for production line productivity, not a thriving collaborative community.

We spent the next few days just walking through most of the questions above. By the second day, without any urging, several participants had already sent draft strategy plans (based on the journey concept) back to their organisations. The whole group was encouraged. "I never thought I'd be able to do strategic planning, but I can do *this*!" Everyone went home with new ideas, a way to dialogue with and include their teams, and a picture of what the future could look like. They did not have lockstep answers or a plan set in concrete, but they had more helpful next steps, options, and goals that could flexibly fit their context. Their journeys were underway.

- Walk through the questions above to begin getting an idea of how to apply the journey concept in your organisation/department/etc. Perhaps you will want to include a few team members to do the exercise with you. Then consider how you would do this on a larger scale.
- Discuss how this approach could help you prepare for the future while remaining flexible.
- Think about how your team could benefit and how this experience might differ from what you've done in the past in the area of strategic planning.

A regional team looks back

We've said that there are no maps for the journey ahead. Traditional strategies set milestones in front of us and mapped out our journey before our feet touched ground. But now we realise we are in new territory. This new landscape requires new ways of thinking, being, and working. We have never been this way before. But how did we get here? We travel by faith and with discernment. But a part of that ongoing discernment process and the resulting wisdom comes from looking to the past. As we look back, our previously uncharted journey can now be charted, and we can see the milestones and reflect on where and how we have been led. We can make maps retracing our past that will give us opportunity for reflection and also help prepare us for the uncharted way forward.

Wycliffe Americas Area leadership requested a strategic review process. A strategic review is usually part of a strategic planning process. It looks at the current state of a company and creates a plan for what needs to happen in order to achieve its goals. Corporations do strategic reviews to evaluate current market conditions, explore opportunities for growth, review how to allocate resources to maximise success, look at strengths and weaknesses, identify changes needed, and determine strategic direction. The standard outcome of a strategic review would ideally be a clear set of strategic recommendations and a future roadmap for the business that charts its course. There are a lot of good intentions in such efforts, but, as many organisations are discovering, the scope and depth of such reviews just isn't enough. And, because such exercises cannot predict the future, yet they establish concrete plans for the future, organisations are often caught off guard. Such are the hazards of drawing maps of unknown territory! Add to these factors that the Americas Area was more of a movement than an institution, and it became apparent that a new kind of review was in order.

Working with the Americas' leadership, we decided that there was much to learn by looking at their history. We chose to look back fifteen years; we gathered six former, current, and up-and-coming leaders and an excellent note-taker, and spent two days in guided conversation. The atmosphere was casual; there was a lot of story-telling and reminiscing, but all stayed focused on the purpose of the gathering. The goal was to: identify, reflect on, document, and share the process, progress, and decisions of the Americas Movement Journey thus far.

The conversation was shaped around these big-picture questions:

- How will the past and present inform the Americas' ongoing journey and future?
- What do you want others to know about the Americas' journey?
- What will help others on their journey?

To help us organise our thoughts, we made sure we covered the following aspects of the journey as part of the discussion:

1. Context: climate, weather, terrain;
2. Identity, vision, values;
3. People;
4. Resources;
5. Principles;
6. Mindset;
7. Decisions;
8. Behaviours;
9. Milestones;
10. Lessons learned;
11. Discernment and goals.

We also clarified the scope of the conversation. We would look back as far as the 1980s to briefly trace the journey that led Wycliffe Americas Area from a largely traditional missions model to becoming a Bible translation movement, involving more than 100 organisations, movements, churches, and denominations in Mexico, Central, and South America. (Canada, the US, and the Caribbean are also part of the Americas Area but were not within the scope of this review.)

- Consider what a journey review process could look like for your team/region/organisation. How might you create a conversation to help you learn from the past and move forward?

To give you an example of what can transpire in such a conversation, here is a sampling of what was explored as we looked at the various aspects of the Americas journey. The bulleted lists and questions can help you create your own conversations.

1. CONTEXT

Consultant participants talked about the "weather": what made the timing right for the movement to happen? What "winds of the Spirit" were blowing? What "rainfall" enriched opportunities and caused growth? What "storms" impeded progress? They also talked about terrain: the significance of geographical locations, and historical, political, sociological, and religious contexts that created opportunities or challenges. They came to the realisation that difficult terrain (geographical and political challenges) and changing weather (new information and data, trends, and movements) together awakened and encouraged new ways of working, more substantial local involvement, and an increasing number of new participants who were better informed than their predecessors.

2. JOURNEY IDENTITY, VISION, VALUES

Articulating the primary motivations for the journey and the beginnings of the journey, participants addressed these questions:

- Where were we then (the Bible translation movements, Wycliffe, the church in the Americas)?
- Where are we now?
- What were the vision and values in the beginning? Have they changed? How? Why?

This was a surprisingly holistic conversation. I've participated in many discussions on identity and values in numerous organisations, many of which hoped for something concrete to emerge. This discussion did not aim to reach concrete statements of identity or values. Still, the resulting list of recognised values not only provided substantial statements but also offered them in helpful contexts that either reflected on the past as they moved forward or acknowledged the deeper reason for the value. The discussion of identity, vision, and values grew organically from the conversations about their journey. There was little "we used to be/do this and now we are/do this". They saw how values grew and changed. They didn't just "switch". The paths and processes were revealed, not just the "befores" and "afters".

Such discussions are much more helpful for evaluating an organisation and for moving forward. You will know where you came from and why. The discussion helped participants see what they valued and what they chose to keep and discard along the way. As one participant stated, they had seen "What moves a movement? Shared vision, values, principles… that's what needs to happen!" This conversation was one of several that demonstrated journey progression exemplified by the participants' commitment to community and to purposefully listening to and following God. These commitments connect their heritage and their future.

3. People

In this conversation, participants explored who had participated with God on the Americas journey and how God had used them. They discussed the following questions:

- Who have the significant leaders and influencers been? Why and how were they leaders and influencers?
- Who were the significant people involved? How has this changed? Why?

The participants honoured a number of their leaders and colleagues in the process of the conversation and noted what they had learned from them and how that could be applied in the future. Much of the discussion happened through storytelling. Although individuals and specific qualities were mentioned, the overall focus of the conversation was on the importance of being a team. Participants could see patterns, changes, and principles that helped them in later conversations about principles and priorities. They could see why they valued specific qualities as they recalled those who had modelled them along the way.

4. Resources

To identify the resources God had provided, participants focused on the following questions:

- What resources have been important? Why?
- How have they been used?
- How were they provided?
- How has thinking about resources changed?
- How has the use of resources changed?

The natural flow of conversation and reflection resulted in the sharing of diverse insights that came together in rich patterns and practical observations. It wasn't a matter of just answering the questions, much less answering them in order. The conversation format allowed participants to visit and revisit topics and questions with further examples and insights along the way. Topics discussed included generosity, nurturing relationships, creativity, control, stewardship priorities, changes in systems and structures, and the overall complexity of the topic of resources. One example was the discussion concerning *efficiency* and how people define it in numerous ways ranging from speed to relationship building.

5. Principles

Principles are guiding rules and beliefs. They are often institutionalised, but in this journey discussion, it became apparent that they genuinely need to be part of the character of the people, not just a part of the structure of the organisation.

Through conversation and storytelling, a pattern emerged of principles related to the value of people and principles representing commitment. Participants looked at reflection and practice, and individual and community responsibilities, and were not trying to make binary choices (such as between simplicity and complexity). Almost every principle also included an implicit agreement to let go of control. Very few of the principles listed could be embraced or enacted by someone bent on power or control.

6. MINDSET

Mindset is a habitual or characteristic mental attitude that determines how a group or person interprets and responds to situations. The team reflected and conversed at length on the past and present and discussed what was needed for continued change and growth in the future. They agreed that mindset significantly affects how individuals or groups approach different scenarios. They dug deep to identify former and still-lingering mindsets and looked at what has changed and why. There was clear evidence of changes that came with reposturing to follow missional intent and a journey mentality. They acknowledged God's control. They stated their own willingness to release control, to change, to grow, to accept that they might not "get it right" every time but that they could still rebound and stay on course and remain committed to participation in God's mission.

7. DECISIONS

Decisions are the specific choices (one-time or ongoing) that have an impact along the way on the journey. Participants discussed the following:

- What were some of the key decisions, and how did they have a significant impact?
- Why did they have an impact? What difference did they make?
- What environment and resources did they require?
- How did they affect the movement's direction, pace, and scope?

Applying the journey approach to this conversation helped participants identify purposeful changes along the journey. They realised very conscious choices were made that took the Americas down a particular path. It wasn't just about inevitable change.

Decisions largely fell into five categories:

- Ground rules;
- Progressive inclusion;
- Rethinking strategy together;
- Choosing community;
- Resource allocation.

An example of the purposeful decisions discussed included:

- Making every structure and process open to examination;
- Removing language barriers in meetings;

- Choosing strategies that would lessen the fears of partners;
- Allowing time and funding to focus on growing friendships;
- Thinking as part of the body rather than as parachurch.

8. Behaviours

Behaviours are how an individual or group acts in various situations. Based on all the earlier conversations, participants were ready to talk about and craft a list of behaviours that characterised the Wycliffe Americas Area people and journey at their best. It was a long list but included observations such as:

- Walk in humility;
- Challenge the status quo;
- Have the attitude of a servant;
- Encourage, grow, and maintain relationships;
- Think outside the box and listen around the world;
- Keep short accounts and deal with rumours;
- Work in collaboration as community.

9. Milestones

A milestone is an action or event marking a significant change in the course of the journey or a stage of development. Milestones may or may not be directly correlated to the abovementioned decisions. They may be tipping points, crises, miracles, crossroads etc. Participants identified key milestones along their journey thus far. In this conversation, they went back as far as the 1930s to add more context. They then created a timeline of the more recent years. It was significant that the milestones offered were focused on people rather than measurements and were primarily connected to relationships and progress in growing and deepening relationships rather than the "industry standard" milestones which focus on goals, metrics, and benchmarks.

10. Lessons learned

This conversation category gave participants the opportunity to discover and articulate what they had learned on the journey thus far. They reflected on and discussed:

- How we learn. "Through trial and error, mistakes, challenging experiences, surprising experiences, the experiences of others…";
- What we now think about differently, do differently, do not do, etc.;
- How these lessons inform the future;
- How we can share these lessons with others;
- God's mission;
- Movements;
- Community;
- Leadership and teams;
- Other.

Among the many lessons learned, one stands out as a message to all of us. "No two people go on exactly the same journey. People trying to do similar things won't have the same journey. Specific lessons are not always helpful, but the principles behind them will be." The participants appreciated the journey review process and wanted to pass on their learnings. They also wanted to clarify that it's a process, not a step-by-step model to follow. Who knows where your conversations will lead!?

11. Discernment and goals

The two-day review ended with conversations on discernment and goals. The participants reflected on all they had discussed as they considered the future and their next steps on the journey.

- What key things do we sense God doing?
- What process of ongoing discernment do we need?
- What should our priorities be?
- What is our vision for the future?
- What are the challenges and opportunities in front of us?

Out of that conversation, there was a natural unfolding of an area focus, global focus, and future focus that included topics that needed attention, opportunities, questions, challenges, and some breakthrough ideas.

One participant's closing comment nicely summed up the experience: "We're a part of something amazing that God has done. We didn't see it coming!" But we can see it and celebrate as we look back, and we can go forward in confidence and faith, better prepared for the journey ahead.

- Remembering that this is a process, not a model, how might a journey-oriented review benefit your team/organisation? Whether or not you decide to pursue the entire process, take time to re-read the bulleted information and discuss, with a few of your team members or your entire team, if and how such conversations might be of help to you.

The goal of this appendix is to give you some practical resources for your own journey, so we have focused on several journey experience examples[3] that may help you on your way. The bullet points and discussion questions are applicable to most organisations, teams, churches, etc., but your own conversations will be unique and – with reflection, prayer, and discernment – can help guide you in the days and years ahead.

---

[3] You can find more in-depth information on the Wycliffe Global Alliance journey thus far and on the case studies presented in this appendix, plus additional case studies, in the book *A Missional Leadership History: the journey from Wycliffe Bible translators... to the Wycliffe Global Alliance.*

Missions always must unfold within the context of, and the anticipation of, God's work, which He alone initiated and which He alone can bring to final completion. This perspective if properly understood, should not render us passive or our work inconsequential. Rather, it puts all of our work within the larger and more ennobling context of God's action and the certainty of final outcome.

Timothy Tennent (2010)